Flexible

Architecture that Responds to Change

Robert Kronenburg

Laurence King Publishing

To: Irene Wilhelmina Kronenburg 1920–2004

LAURENCE KING

Published in 2007 by
Laurence King Publishing Ltd
e-mail: enquiries@laurenceking.co.uk
www.laurenceking.co.uk

Text © 2007 Robert Kronenburg
This book was designed and produced by
Laurence King Publishing Ltd, London

A catalogue record for this book is available
from the British Library

ISBN-13: 978 1 85669 461 2
ISBN-10: 1 85669 461 5

Designed by Godfrey Design. www.godfreydesign.co.uk
Printed in China.

Cover: Allianz Arena, Munich, Germany,
2005: Herzog and De Meuron
p.5 (top): Matsumoto Performing
Arts Centre, Matsumoto, Japan,
2004: Toyo Ito
p.5 (bottom): Strandbeest, the
Netherlands, 2003–5: Theo Jansen
pp.8–9: Curtain Wall House, Tokyo,
Japan, 1995: Shigeru Ban
pp.112–13: Halley VI Antarctica
Base, project 2005: Hugh Broughton
Architects/FaberMaunsell Ltd

Contents

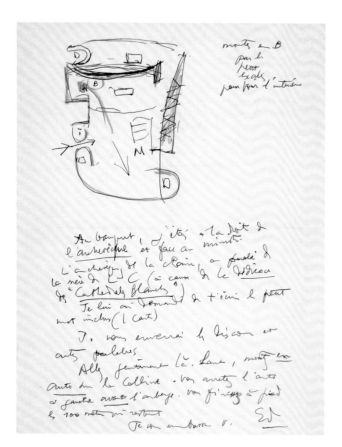

Sketch of the plan, Notre Dame
du Haut, Ronchamp, France, 1955:
Le Corbusier.

Foreword

When I was still a student, shortly after completing my
first year in architectural practice, I took a long trip through
Europe. 'Interail' (a cross-network rail ticket that lasted for
a month, or more if you had the stamina) was the most
affordable transport method at that time and gave the bearer
unlimited travel on all the railway systems of Western
Europe, and also some in Eastern Europe. Those on a budget
– myself included – typically stretched their limited funds by
not only using the trains for travel, but also for resting and
sleeping. As the journey wore on, trains were not necessarily

selected by where they ended up, but rather by when they left
and how long they took. By this method, a night's sleep might,
though not always, be obtained.

On long trips passengers made friends (and enemies),
played games, learnt convenient languages, rested, read and
slept. We cooked meals and prepared endless cups of tea with
our camping stove on the compartment floor. Couchettes, seats,
floors and luggage racks all became temporary beds. I recall
one train stopping at a lonely place in the middle of the night
and a border guard, with a machine-gun, becoming distinctly
twitchy when a fellow traveller poked his head out from
where he was sleeping on the floor beneath the bank of seats
in our compartment. Over an extended trip, the train became
a slow-moving essay in how people are able to make do, carry
on with their lives and adapt in clearly unsuitable conditions.

Though not the longest journey, the one I recall with
greatest intensity was from Paris to Ronchamp in south-east
France. Leaving Gare Montparnasse late in the evening,
the train rattled overnight through dark countryside to its
destination. Changing to a local line at Belfort station in the
small hours I found the carriage dark and not due to leave for
an hour or more. Falling asleep, I finally woke to a dreamlike,
rocking motion as the little train pulled into Ronchamp
station. Le Corbusier's chapel of Notre Dame du Haut was,
of course, the reason for my pilgrimage to this part of rural
France. From the station, it was a long walk up a steep hill
to the building, but what a magnificent arrival. Shortly after
dawn, the setting of the building among hills and forests
was unforgettable with the mist rising and birds singing –
I sat on top of an adjacent monument and made tea.

After hours of being on my own with the building, the
priest finally arrived and opened up the church. I went inside
to an entirely contemporary, though simultaneously timeless,
space. Lit only by the coloured glass windows and a line
of candles near the altar, the interior seemed pure and
simple yet also infinitely complex – an amorphous, organic
interpretation of spirituality. As I stood there another small
group of visitors arrived, wandered quietly around in the
mostly empty space and, without any obvious signal, began
to sing in unison. The space, already incredibly powerful,
resonated with sound, which, when added to the light and the
volume and form of the architecture, created one of the most
powerful architectural experiences of my life.

Le Corbusier, a man ostensibly without religious
affiliation, created a rich, symbolic, spiritual space that
challenges the ritual and formality that places of worship
usually rely on. In so doing he has allowed movement, sound
and light to contact the essence of human senses. The wonder
of this architecture is in its situation, like an ancient stone
circle or earthwork; in its solid, yet responsive, form; in its
ambiguous, yet receptive, image; and also in its capacity to

allow unpredictable things to take place within a loose and adaptable interior. An architect who was responsible, more than most, for creating a deterministic and pedagogical movement during much of his career returned, in this and other masterly late projects, to his early pursuit of responsive humanistic building.

Though this is just one event that led to my early and continuing interest in responsive and adaptable architecture, it was also at this time that I had my own first engagement in this field after winning a competition for a mobile exhibition facility. Along with two colleagues, I spent a year overseeing it being built and then in operation around the UK. Later, I also became involved in the design of temporary buildings for special events and commercial systems. These possessed a great ingenuity and flexibility, though they lacked formal architectural credibility. At the time, the general understanding was that flexible buildings had their uses, but that they were also quite limited – this sort of design was seen as less important than permanent, fixed architecture. As I have learnt, and I hope this book shows, this general presumption could and should be challenged. Mobile, adaptable and flexible design is well placed not only to solve a wide range of architectural problems, but to do it better than more conventional responses.

Flexible architecture consists of buildings that are designed to respond easily to change throughout their lifetime. The benefits of this form of design can be considerable: it remains in use longer; fits its purpose better; accommodates users' experience and intervention; takes advantage of technical innovation more readily; and is economically and ecologically more viable. It also has greater potential to remain relevant to cultural and social trends. This book explores the cultural context of flexible architecture, its history as a distinct genre of building design and, through the examination of recently built projects, focuses on the characteristics that may be of value in the creation of a new generation of contemporary, flexible building designs.

One project that this book examines in detail is Toyo Ito's Matsumoto Performing Arts Centre in Japan (2004). A few weeks after this building was opened I was able to meet with Ito in his Tokyo office to discuss his recent work on new projects in Japan and Europe. Of the many things that we talked about, one in particular stood out. Ito described how many of his earlier buildings had been designed in the modernist tradition in which he was trained. The aspiration in this form of architecture is to create a lightness of geometry and minimalism by taking away more and more 'non-essential' features in order to achieve a state of purity. In a wonderfully frank and perceptive statement Ito explained that although this created undeniable beauty, it had become clear to him that at some point this meant that people would also be taken away. He had therefore developed a parallel design route that had now taken precedence in his work – the search for a fluid architecture that only becomes complete once people inhabit and use the building. This aspiration is a key principle in the generation of flexible architecture. Good designers who attempt to respond to flexible agendas use all the tools that they can find to solve their problem.

Part I of this book is an overview of the intermingling agendas of flexible architecture. It explores the historical context that has shaped contemporary design and the changes in society and culture that may eventually lead to its next incarnation. It examines the crucial role of the house as an exemplar for architectural progress; the impact that flexible design can have on public buildings and the urban situation; and the strategies that are forming its emergence as a distinct genre.

Part II is organized around four characteristics of flexible architecture: adaptation; transformation; movability; and interaction. 'Adapt' includes buildings that are designed to adjust to different functions, users and climate change. It is architecture that has a loose fit and is sometimes called 'open building'. 'Transform' includes buildings that change shape, space, form or appearance by the physical alteration of their structure, skin or internal surfaces. It is architecture that opens, closes, expands and contracts. 'Move' includes buildings that relocate from place to place in order to fulfil their function better – it is architecture that rolls, floats or flies. 'Interact' includes buildings that respond to user's requirements in automatic or intuitive ways. It is architecture that uses sensors to initiate changes in appearance and environment or operation that are enabled by kinetic systems and intelligent materials. It is important to note, however, that because good designers take advantage of all the strategies that are available to address the issues, in only very few cases can a building be placed within just one of these areas – these are therefore themes rather than categories.

Although I have been exploring this general topic for two decades, I began dedicated work on this book in 2000 when I was invited to advise on the curation of the Vitra exhibition, *Living in Motion*. I am grateful to Mathias Schwartz-Clauss and Alexander von Vegesack for involving me in this exciting project. As I write, this wonderful exhibition continues to tour the world more than three years after it was first opened. I must also gratefully acknowledge the UK Arts and Humanities Research Council for providing a research study leave grant that greatly helped me to find precious research and writing time. Finally, I must thank Philip Cooper, John Jervis and Laurence King Publishing for their commitment and engagement with the project.

Robert Kronenburg,
Liverpool School of Architecture

Part 1

Introduction

Human beings are flexible creatures. We move about at will, manipulate objects and operate in a wide range of environments. There was a time, not too long ago in evolutionary terms, when our existence was based on our capacity for movement and adaptability; indeed it is to this that we owe our survival as a species. Most cultures now lead a more or less sedentary life, but it could be that flexibility is once again becoming a priority in human development and that technological, social and economic changes are forcing, or at least encouraging, a new form of nomadic existence based on global markets, the world wide web and cheap, fast transportation.

The North African Bedouin tent is still used in many different forms, but essentially it is a tensile membrane suspended from compression poles. It is mobile and light-weight yet still adaptable to a harsh climate, coping with extreme environmental changes.

The *Yurta* or *Ger* is a manufactured building from Central Asia in which the separate parts are manufactured by specialists. It incorporates a geodetic wall structure and compression and tension rings in the roof. The building is usually dismantled for transportation but has sufficient strength to be carried over shorter distances.

This book explores the concept of flexible living by examining the type of built environment that can help us to sustain life on the move. It examines the genesis of flexible design in traditional and historic building patterns and explores, in greater detail, recent architecture from the beginnings of the modern to the present day. Primarily, though, it focuses on an examination of the contemporary buildings and prototypes that are not only responding to today's problems but are also predicting the architecture of tomorrow.

Flexible buildings are intended to respond to changing situations in their use, operation or location. This is architecture that adapts, rather than stagnates; transforms, rather than restricts; is motive, rather than static; interacts with its users, rather than inhibits. It is a design form that is, by its very essence, cross-disciplinary and multi-functional; consequently it is frequently innovative and expressive of contemporary design issues. However, flexible architecture is not a new phenomenon, but a form of building that has evolved alongside human beings' developing creative skills. It has a long and fascinating history that is intrinsically linked with the development of architectural form. Where functional problems have necessitated a responsive, built environment, flexible architecture has formed at least a part of the solution. The factors that have forged its development reinforce the value and relevancy of flexible architecture as a response to contemporary problems associated with technological, social and economic change.

Surprisingly, most people are used to architecture that is essentially composed of static, solid objects – the possibilities of completely flexible buildings, however, are limitless. For example, consider a house that has been specifically designed to offer changing opportunities to its inhabitants – the option to have peace and seclusion while living in the centre of the city, or to be connected to friends and business colleagues while living in a remote place. It could be a house designed for a single person during the week and for six at the weekend, or a home that you took with you on business trips. Perhaps a building that fits your individual needs now, but one that you can invest in over the course of your life and divide up between your children to give them each a starter home when they need it. Flexible architecture might create an environment that automatically responds to your every need or one that requires you not to be too comfortable, to try living in a different way and to force adaptability and change on yourself.

The ultimate flexible interior may be one that is completely amorphous and transitional; changing shape, colour, lighting level, acoustics and temperature as the inhabitant moves through it – abandoning flat horizontal surfaces and demarcations between hard and soft, warm and cold, wet and dry. A flexible building could be architecture as installation, assembled at a site at a particular time for a particular purpose – architecture as assignation, an agreement between family, colleagues and friends to become joint occupants when they meet together at a certain point in time and space. It could be a structure that is lightly placed in the landscape of our cities and countryside, rather than founded there, allowing the physical environment to continue around it, subtly and perhaps only temporarily affected by its presence. It could be a house that interacts with the surrounding landscape in a less formal sense and becomes an event rather than an object. It could be an architecture that depends, for its character, as much on the changing combinations of its surrounding environment (both buildings and landscapes) as on its own form.

Most of today's architecture is not like this. Though in previous millennia we may have been accustomed to a nomadic existence, moving with the seasons, transporting light-weight, mobile, multi-use home-made tools (including buildings) with us, we are now accustomed to living and working in static, mostly standardized environments. They are built to the lowest common denominator for (apparently) standardized people, carrying out standard functions. Homes are mostly chosen from speculative builders, offices from speculative developers and factories from a range of sizes and locations that are coded with letters and numbers.

Building is primarily a mass-produced industry, although it still struggles to achieve the real benefits of mass-production (such as efficiencies in production and delivery), with industry leaders continuously making basic assumptions about the range of activities and operating parameters for most building types, with the prime objective of cutting costs. As with all mass-production it is hard to accommodate variety, specificity and change in its products. However, buildings are different from other complex, mass-produced items, such as cars, for a range of important reasons.

Buildings have a long and complicated life, during which their parameters of use can change widely. They are mostly built on permanent sites, but the environment around them continues to change as other buildings are redeveloped or replaced. Streets, neighbourhoods and indeed whole cities can change character – from commercial to residential and from industrial to entertainment, then back again. The way buildings are actually used can also alter dramatically. For example, the building function might change – warehouse to dwelling, shop to office. Even if its basic purpose remains unchanged, the way that purpose is carried out can develop beyond recognition. As the provision of building facilities is the greatest investment supporting human activity, architectural development and redevelopment should be as efficient as possible. Therefore, the capacity to accommodate change could be the most important factor in determining economic efficiency and performance in sustainability terms.

The *Tipi* emerged as a response to the need for the rapid provision of shelter when the introduction of the horse heralded a shift to a nomadic culture for the Native American tribes. Compression poles create a conic form from which is draped a non-structural membrane.

There is no doubt that economic, efficiency and sustainability issues are important, but there is something else that is perhaps even more critical in determining the success or failure of architectural development. In his influential essay, 'Building, Dwelling, Thinking', the German philosopher Martin Heidegger described how human beings recognize and establish a sense of place. In Heidegger's example, a bridge (which he uses rather than a building in order to define the act of creation as a rite of passage) is not a place; it only brings a place into existence. 'The place did not exist before the bridge … Thus, the bridge is not a place in itself but it is only from the bridge that the place originates.'[1] Heidegger's belief is that places are brought into existence by something more than the act of building. Though the essence of place is supported by this costly and time-consuming act, a place can also be brought into existence by much simpler acts, such as rearranging the furniture in a room or even unpacking a suitcase!

In some cultures the act of place-making is achieved with even more flexible, ephemeral acts than this. In the Japanese landscape there are many instances where place-making is not associated with buildings, but is achieved by the act of 'binding' – encircling trees, rocks, even apparently empty places with rope, fabric and paper. In Aboriginal Australian culture, a place can be defined by travelling along a prescribed route that has been recounted in a story. These circumstances show that a place is not necessarily achieved by the creation of a permanent building and that movable and temporary artefacts and situations can be equally significant. Western sensitivities are no less aware of this possibility. The temporary identification of a significant place by the placing of flowers and messages as a memorial to someone who has died, for example in a road traffic accident, is evidence of this.

In his essay, however, Heidegger made it clear that the act of building is the most important way of creating a sense of dwelling in the world. For the Japanese, the indigenous Australians and in fact for everyone, the act of making a home, a place to work or to relax, is something we do along the way. It is a transient and continuously developing act. As the German-born academic Günter Nitschke eloquently states, 'Place is the product of lived space and lived time.'[2] All this would suggest that individuals need buildings that are responsive to their needs; therefore buildings for any purpose would better suit us if they had a significant degree of adaptability, flexibility and capacity for change.

All buildings can accommodate some change, but most have a specific number of rooms of set sizes with fixed openings – the doors, windows and closets open and close, but little else does. Though every building has the possibility for some further degree of flexibility, it requires significant effort, inconvenience and expenditure to release it by

Bound space, Kumano Nyakuoji, Kyoto, Japan.

Shugakuin Rakushi-ken and
Shugakuin Kyusvi-tei, Kyoto, Japan:
Shugakuin Rikyu Imperial Villa was
completed in 1659 for the former
Emperor Gomizuno-o. These smaller
buildings within the landscape
complex indicate the traditional
Japanese ideal of formal simplicity
coupled with ultimate flexibility in
use of space and integration with
the external environment.

altering, converting or extending – usually to provide yet
more inflexible space. So, what might a more flexible building
be like? A building designed for responsive living could be one
that, during its occupation, might be moved from one place to
another or changed in shape or structure – the walls might
fold; floors shift; staircases extend; lighting, colours and
surface textures metamorphose. Parts of the building could
extend or even leave the site completely, or the entire facility
could roll, float or fly to a different location.

Is such responsive architecture necessary? Human
physiological needs are simple: to be warm and to have
enough food and drink. We can extend this to our
psychological needs: to feel safe and wanted. The success of
the human race lies in our ability to be flexible. Although we
can cope with all kinds of privations, a part of our success is
also our inbuilt need for change and improvement. Setting
ambitions and achieving them is a vital component in human
nature – we desire to have the best possible food, artefacts
and environment. Like every other aspect of human
achievement the design of buildings is subject to continuous
change, with the ambition of making improvements. A mobile,
adaptable, transformable building could be wonderful in the
true sense of the word: full of wonder – a magical stage that
would allow dramatically different activities to occur within
the same, but changing, space.

The requirement for flexibility stems not just from
desire and possibility, but also from economy and necessity.
Since humankind first came into existence we have been
nomadic creatures, leading lives that are closely bound to the
movement of the wild animals that fed and clothed us. Even
when we had domesticated animals, we still moved according
to seasonal grazing, and when humans finally settled to
longer-term habitation (villages, towns and cities), a few
rooms of each dwelling were multi-functional – used for
sleeping, eating, entertaining and sometimes work.
Consequently, these rooms were furnished with demountable
tables, stools and benches; chests containing clothes also
served as seats. Sleep has always had special significance
as a human activity in which we become separate from our
normal state of consciousness, and so there are dedicated
symbolic and practical bed designs. However, because human
beings are adaptable creatures, tables, benches and chests
have also been commonly utilized as elevated sleeping platforms.

Even when large portions of society became
sedentary, their existence was still dependent on a
significant group of specialist travellers who maintained
a nomadic lifestyle. Caravan drivers, herders and drovers,
sailors, merchants and warriors were all professions that
were introduced or whose role was enhanced. The traditional
purpose of a nomadic way of life was to make the best use
of scant resources; however these new forms of travelling

The Tithe Barn, Great Coxwell, UK, built by Cistercian monks in the early fourteenth century.

lifestyles emerged in response both to increased agricultural and technological skills and to new demands for services and products. They also resulted in the development of appropriate flexible and mobile shelters and artefacts.

It is only in the last three centuries in Europe that rooms with dedicated functions and specifically associated furniture have appeared.[3] In Japan, however, a flexible mode of living continues to the present day, partly by convention, partly due to the lack of space in many urban homes. The modern Japanese family home has at least one tatami room, where flexible items of furniture and fittings are introduced, moved around and removed as required. The same room may be used as a social space, a private retreat and a sleeping space. People sit on the floor on cushions that sometimes have back or arm rests, low tables are used for working or sometimes eating and futons are rolled out for sleeping. Often stairway/storage cupboards are movable pieces of furniture that connect floor levels. To live in such a home is to engage with it in a far more meaningful way than just switching on a light or opening a window. It is to rearrange your surroundings according to mood and circumstance – whether you need an object-free space for solitude and relaxation or to put out items of comfort and consideration for when visitors arrive.

Though the home is undoubtedly the root of all architecture, specialist building functions that have subsequently been developed also follow the historical pattern of multi-purpose, flexible structures that have gradually given way to more specialized uses. There is, however, one exception. Whereas early, non-domestic buildings were created with multi-functional spaces that could accommodate a range of farming activities, religious structures were highly specialized, with specific spaces that were closely identified with rituals and imagery. Hard-won resources were used sparingly and efficiently for functional needs, but used lavishly on dedicated religious and, later, civic buildings that represented status and power. Not surprisingly, it is these permanent, static structures that have created the legacy that, until recently, has formed the main source for architectural history – a chronological story of styles that have supplanted each other through the centuries. It was only in the twentieth century that recognition of the value, beauty and elegance of non-pedigreed architecture emerged through the work of anthropologists, such as Amos Rapoport, and architectural historians, such as Bernard Rudofsky and Paul Oliver.[4]

There have, however, always been buildings that are required for functional, pragmatic work. These have consequently been created with a functional elegance that has allowed them to cope with change. The great European, medieval tithe barns were built as seasonal storage containers, but also found use as shelters for animals, implements and activities – they provided places to gather for social functions and for entertainment. In the nineteenth century, British manufacturers developed prefabricated building systems that enabled a wide range of administrative, industrial and residential buildings to be shipped to locations all over the world. Mobile military buildings have been used for centuries as shelters, places for meetings and for the manufacture and maintenance of weapons in the field. However, as campaigns became more complex new facilities emerged, such as canteens and hospitals. By the early twentieth century a range of mobile building systems had been developed that included easily transported, large-span structures that could be used as vehicle sheds and even aircraft hangars. The realm of entertainment is yet another area to have been influenced by the need for more flexible accommodation. The first circuses and travelling carnivals were originally held in local farm buildings; however, by the nineteenth century sophisticated, mobile entertainment buildings had been created to provide larger, more suitable venues. These examples are just a small selection of the wide range of flexible structures that have been developed in parallel with their static counterparts. As dedicated building types have emerged to more closely deliver the services necessary in contemporary society, flexible ones have emerged alongside also to cater to changing needs.

Workable flexible architecture can be found in every sphere of human activity – commerce, industry, education, medicine, military and entertainment – but the vast majority of western architecture is static, of single purpose and with standardized furniture and fittings. So why is this? The reason is circumstantial and, it would seem, has more to do with recent economic cultural history than with the character of human personality or the responsive requirements that we can now identify in contemporary architecture. Though building development takes place around an infrastructure that appears to consist of unmoving objects – roads, bridges, and site boundaries – the perception that this is an apparently continuous and unchanging backdrop is untrue.

Change constantly takes place as economic, social and cultural pressures impact on both building development and infrastructural needs. Society is never static; human civilization has an integral tendency towards change – usually towards progress and improvements in the condition of human existence. Consequently, the impact of this on the built environment is manifest: roads are extended and re-routed; services repaired, improved and reinstated; buildings demolished and rebuilt. The first outward indication of an emerging nation's changing economic status is the erection of buildings, often of some identifiable significant status. Thomas Walter's 1863 Capitol building in nineteenth-century Washington, USA can be compared to Cesar Pelli's late twentieth-century Petronas Towers (1998) in Kuala Lumpur, Malaysia in this way.

The Harlequin Circus, located in Liverpool, UK, continues the imagery of the 'big top' using contemporary materials, structural systems and erection techniques. The caravans of performers and crew form a temporary village with its own high street illuminated by car-park lighting.

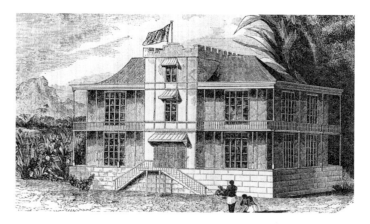

The Iron Palace, 1843: a colonial prefabricated building, designed and manufactured in Britain for King Eyambo, Calabar River, Nigeria for assembly on site.

In this whirlwind of change it is a natural inclination to seek stability; however, stability is relative. Though we perceive buildings as the longest-lasting manifestation of human activity, these too are constantly changing and at great cost because they are created using a process that requires destruction before construction can take place again. This is wasteful in building resources, ecologically damaging and inefficient in terms of placing the facility out of use for substantial periods. Nevertheless, this method of responding to change has been the norm for centuries, virtually without challenge. This is a remarkable conundrum: human ingenuity, which is primarily directed towards doing things in the most efficient and economic way, continues to employ a process that is manifestly inefficient – why? In essence, it would appear that this is because, although buildings are perceived as a usable resource, the underlying agenda is that they are created as a form of investment.

The ownership of land is a key factor in establishing wealth. Once land is owned, the emphasis is on how that land can be made to increase in value – this is usually achieved by making it more desirable. Land and building together become 'property' and property is not architecture, or even building, but investment. The value of investment lies in its stability, not in flux, so development that has a predictable, fixed outcome leads to a more stable investment. Buildings that are built for investment do not necessarily even need to have a user – speculative building is carried out constantly without prospective users having been identified. Consequently they are built to design principles that establish a lowest common denominator – one size fits all.

Paradoxically, building for an unknown future user could be a driver towards better flexible architecture. Instead, however, it tends to lead to the antithesis of building for change because, instead of being open to being used by whoever has most need (social or commercial), the type of user is determined by investment potential – typically office, luxury apartment or retail. Programmatic design in speculative development is therefore strictly defined. The design and manufacture of buildings is, of course, associated with needs, aspirations and predictions, but the principal underlying driver is economics; what will prove to be the best financial investment over time.

Despite this, world economics, like everything else, is subject to continual change. In the light of these changes, therefore, is it reasonable that the vast majority of buildings remain no more than a symbol of appropriation? What are the building needs of today? How far are they a universal problem as opposed to one governed by site, climate, culture, economics and regulations? Certainly, the global movement of population has become a universal constant. Most usually it is individuals that relocate, change jobs, cities and social groupings. However, more and more frequently large groups of people are forced

Mobile hospital designed by British company Calvert and Light for the Crimea campaign, 1860.

Prefabricated World War II airfield by the Butler Company. The hangars, workshops, housing (based on Buckminster Fuller's Domestic Dwelling Unit [DDU]) and even the prefabricated runway could all be manufactured by the Butler Company in its US factories.

to move as a result of enormous, sometimes catastrophic, economic, social or natural circumstances, such as famines, wars and earthquakes. In these circumstances the permanent building seems to be anomalous – the initial requirement is for shelter to sustain life, protection from the elements and a hygienic space for medical aid. This is closely followed by sustainable aid that supports the refugees in devising their own solution. Unfortunately, many groups often exist for months, or even years, in a political limbo and without a location where more permanent communities can be resuscitated. When people can safely return to their home locality, support is needed in helping them to rebuild in a way that will make their new buildings resist future disasters.[5]

Shelter after disaster brings special problems of its own, but even in less extreme situations the approach to securing a usable building is increasingly ephemeral – shelter may be rented, squatted and, as discussed earlier, purchased as some sort of temporary investment forming the collateral for some future move. The place in which we live and work, rather than being a specific geographic location, is more and more about a set of personal activities, habits and relationships than an established continuum of habitation in the same location. Communications technology has accelerated this trend, fostering the possibilities for tele-working – direct contact with employers, customers and even friends is becoming less of a necessity and more of a luxury. In addition, technology is bringing a new range of opportunities in terms of how we build. New materials are emerging that are lighter, more durable and more easily made into complex shapes. Consequently, these are affecting the shape, form, colour and texture of buildings. Simultaneously, there is a growing awareness of the significant impact that design has on the way we live. Individual products that make life easier, safer or more enjoyable are beginning to be perceived as extensions of our lifestyle. An appreciation of the built environment as an equally malleable extension of who we are and how we live has a direct correlation with this phenomenon.

There is also growing awareness that what we do now will affect our future. National and global legislation, instigated by public demand, is therefore pushing for a greater adherence to ecological and sustainability criteria. The issue of how humanity dwells in the world and makes use of its resources is now on both our individual and government agendas. People want the best quality of life for themselves now, but there is also an increasing awareness that this should be shared with all of humanity, and that there are limited resources with which to achieve this.

Our innate ability to adapt and change is a core element in shaping how our environment can continue to be developed with an increased response to these emerging environmental

The Hankyu Department Store, Osaka, Japan is a mixed-use shopping/entertainment experience in which a Ferris wheel passes through the main atrium of the building.

factors. We are beginning to realise that work is something that can be done in different ways and in different places, that the need to be in a specific place continuously to carry out work may not be necessary. Buildings once had to be sited together in specific places to fulfil their function. These days, many types of work can now be done remotely from places of manufacture or commerce. Facilities that once had to be provided in a fixed location in order to operate can, and in some cases must, be provided in different places in order to work effectively. Spaces that were once provided for a lifetime of use in a dedicated function must now be designed for changing uses and users. Infrastructure that was once built to respond to static situations now needs to be responsive to changing situations. All these things have to be done, not only without compromising performance, but also by using fewer resources in construction, operating and maintenance.

The imperatives that drive what and how we build are under more pressure now than at any time since the Industrial Revolution. Even investment economies have recognized this fact in the emergence of the 'dotcom' business boom that was built, not on precious metals, industrial products or solid structures in city centres, but on flexible, ephemeral information brought instantly to any location.

The features of contemporary life that lead to mobility – personal transportation, computing, mobile phones and access to affordable air travel – are directly linked to the economic, political, social, demographic and technological developments that are now taken for granted in the West, but which are rapidly spreading to other parts of the world. Increased prosperity in Eastern Europe, Asia and India will undoubtedly lead to the same pressures that have resulted in dramatic changes in the way people live in Europe and North America. For example, these regions are already documented as becoming subject to the phenomenon of 'pluralization of lifestyle', where the conventional family is replaced by more fluid groupings that differ in size and make-up and are subject to more frequent change.[6] The societal impact of change is fast becoming a global phenomenon.

Despite these pressures, any new form of flexible architecture does still share the same requirements that all architecture must fulfil. Architecture has certain timeless qualities that represent a stable, developing society and help to establish continuity and purpose. Flexible architecture must respond to new problems and opportunities that arise from cultural, societal and functional needs. It also has to provide meaningful, high-quality design in fulfilling the human desire for meaning and beauty. Though change is driving its development, it must still respond in a balanced way to the constant theatres in which human activity takes place – in our private and public lives, at home and in the community – each of which contributes to our sense of how we dwell in the world.

Osaka neon, Japan: a physical manifestation of a fast-moving, multi-cultural, media and technology focused society.

1 Martin Heidegger, 'Building, Dwelling, Thinking' (1951) in David Krell (ed.), *Martin Heidegger, Basic Writings*, London, 1993, p.347.
2 Günter Nitschke, *From Shinto to Ando: Studies in Architectural Anthropology in Japan*, London, 1993, p.49.
3 For a history of the development of the western domestic interior see Witold Rybczynski, *Home: A Short History of an Idea*, New York, 1987.
4 Amos Rapoport, *House Form and Culture*, New Jersey, 1969; Bernard Rudofsky, *Architecture Without Architects*, New York, 1964; Paul Oliver, *Shelter and Society*, London, 1969.
5 For a detailed examination of the use of mobile structures for shelter after disaster see Robert Kronenburg, *Houses in Motion: The Genesis, History and Development of the Portable Building*, second edition, Chichester, 2002, pp.101–7.
6 Antje Flade, 'Psychological Considerations of Dwelling' in Mathias Schwartz-Clauss (ed.), *Living in Motion: Design and Architecture for Flexible Dwelling*, Weil-am-Rhein, 2002, pp.220–37.

Flexible Home

Ové Glas House, Sweden, 2004: 24H.

The twentieth-century design breakthrough into modernism can be charted through the design of one-off houses. The progressive British Arts and Crafts movement provided the foundation for a range of European styles that were to follow – Art Nouveau, Art Deco, *Jugendstil* and the Viennese Secession. In the years following the First World War, the house was a crucial model for exploring new ideas about lifestyle and the implementation of innovative technology. It remains the definitive architectural vehicle, simultaneously a tool and a symbol that can convey new ideas about a vast range of concepts ranging from the pragmatic to the esoteric. Our understanding of what a house is meant to do provides a baseline beside which innovation can be tested – it enables us to explore everything from new constructional and structural systems to experimental social grouping. The house is the 'laboratory, test-tube and Petri dish of new forms, technologies and living patterns.'[1] It is an important design exemplar for all architecture, not just dwelling, and a powerful tool in the architect's armoury when communicating various new ideas from construction techniques to urban design and aesthetic form.[2]

Frank Lloyd Wright, while building up his experience in Louis Sullivan's innovative Chicago-based architectural practice, saw the new stylistic developments in Europe in domestic and imported journals. He was also exposed to the work of the US informal 'Shingle'-style architects and influences from further away, including the three traditional buildings that were erected by Japanese craftsmen at the 1893 Columbia Exposition. The flowing space and unfettered integration with the site that was afforded by sliding walls and open-plan design, and the sensitivity to natural materials and resolution within a modular, tatami-mat layout, undoubtedly made a big impression on Wright. His understanding of Japanese architecture was further boosted by a three-month visit to the country in 1905.

From 1895, Wright had developed his Prairie-style domestic architecture that aimed to establish a relationship with nature, comfort and modernity. These buildings, though varying enormously in detail, incorporated several common characteristics. In the living areas, space flowed uninterrupted, usually around the focus of a substantial fireplace – the heart of a house in the cold Midwest winters. The walls were permeated, if not by a completely movable screen (which was to appear later in western architecture), then at least by a continuous line of glazed shutters that provided both a view of the surrounding landscape and allowed cooling breezes into the house. Large overhanging eaves shaded the houses from the hot summer sun and also contributed to the low, linear appearance that enhanced an impression of connection with the earth.

In 1909, Wright travelled through Europe, cooperating along the way with the German publisher Ernst Wasmuth A.G. to create a portfolio of his buildings and designs. *Ausgeführte Bauten und Entwürfe von Frank Lloyd Wright* was published in 1910. This, and the subsequent more affordable book version, were widely distributed and owned or at least seen by each of the emerging modernist designers including Peter Behrens, Le Corbusier, Walter Gropius, Mies van der Rohe and Otto Wagner.[3] Wright's work set the foundation for the revolution in domestic architecture that was to come – in subsequent years he developed the idea of the Prairie House into the Usonian House, a simple, affordable, modular, open-plan building type using modern building techniques in partnership with traditional materials. He even envisaged a new urban prototype, Broadacre City, in which the freely available land that was a characteristic of the US Midwest was occupied by settlements of such buildings, each on their own personally tended garden plot. His vision of a decentralized and increasingly mobile suburban society based on individual houses set on their own plot and linked by the automobile could hardly be more different from that of his European contemporaries.

Robie House, Chicago, USA, 1911: Frank Lloyd Wright.

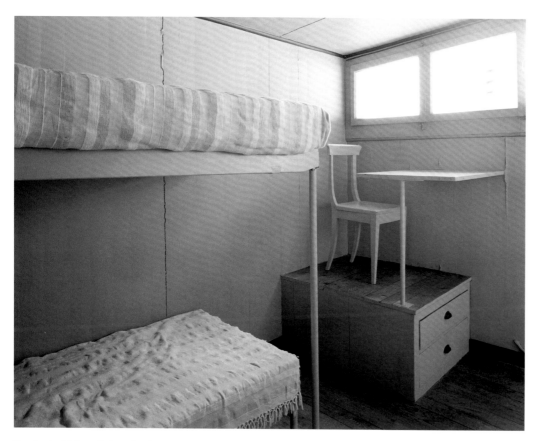

Une Petite Maison, Switzerland, 1923–4: Le Corbusier.

Nevertheless, it was Europe that was to be the main scene for the revolution in architecture that began in the first half of the twentieth century. The architectural language that was promoted by Le Corbusier became known as the International Style – *piloti*, ribbon windows, a wall and plan layout unrestricted by structure, and flat usable roofs. Its promoters heralded it as liberation from the dictatorship of historicism, though it did not necessarily make for more adaptable, or even inhabitable, houses. However, Le Corbusier's best work, such as the masterpiece Villa Savoye (1930), created a merging of spaces with an almost cinematic quality that encouraged and rewarded personal movement via a succession of ramps and volumes. It cannot be denied that such interlocking living areas are an essential element of flexible space.

One of his earliest buildings, Une Petite Maison (1923–4), indicates his receptiveness, particularly in his early projects, to the desirability of adaptable design. This small, single-storey building was built on the shores of Lake Geneva in Switzerland as a retirement home for his parents. Created as a minimal home, perfectly suited to the lives of the two people he knew so well, it was primarily the intermittent visits of the son that necessitated the flexible elements in the design, such as a gridded, folding and sliding screen to create a temporary separate guest area and an extending dinner table to accommodate extra diners. Le Corbusier also designed much of the furniture that is woven into the form of the building, including a composite chest of drawers that forms a platform and elevated desk related to a high-level window that overlooks the lake.

Other liveable and flexible modern buildings were created during this period, notably E-1027 (1926–9), the house designed and built by Eileen Gray in Roquebrune-Cap-Martin, France, and the Van der Leeuw House (1928–9) in Rotterdam by Jan Brinkman and Cornelis van der Vlugt. The Van der Leeuw House featured entire walls of glass that swung up and over to connect the inside of the house directly to the outside. There was even a retracting glass roof above a solarium and extractor fans, bathroom taps, light fittings and curtains that were electrically activated by remote control.[4]

E-1027 was Eileen Gray's first completed work of architecture, though she was an accomplished interior and furniture designer. She collaborated with her partner, Jean Badovici, on the building (the name of the house is a coded linking of their names), but he left most of the design decisions to her. Though the house is clearly within the modernist canon, it expresses a different sensibility to how the inhabitant would interact with the environment. She had little time for the theories that placed architecture as a formal composition above the needs of the user, and in

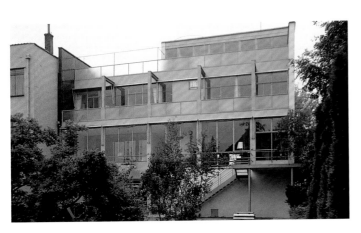

Van der Leeuw House, Rotterdam, the Netherlands, 1928–9: Jan Brinkman and Cornelis van der Vlugt.

E-1027, Roquebrune-Cap-Martin, France, 1926–9: Eileen Gray.

describing the house stated: 'lyricism can lose itself in the play of volumes, in the light of day, [however] the interior should still respond to man's needs, and to the exigencies and needs of individual life'.[5] E-1027 incorporated many special design elements that blurred the line between what was building and what was furniture – desks, tables, chairs and cupboards folded and slid from the house's walls and surfaces. The principal *salle* was a multi-purpose space that was living room, wardrobe, dining area, bar and a guest room, complete with bed and shower. The other rooms were smaller, but also had interlinking functions – each internal space related to a private exterior for the views and also to extend the room's volume. This was a modernist architecture that focused on human experience as a primary generator in creating form.

Perhaps the most famous flexible domestic environment of this period is the Rietveld Schröder House in Utrecht, designed in 1924 by De Stijl architect Gerrit Rietveld in collaboration with his client and lover, Truus Schröder-Schräder. The ground floor is more conventionally planned, but the upper storey of the house was designed to reflect Schröder's romantic image of Bohemian one-room living, while also responding to practical needs with the introduction of partitionable spaces that could be utilized at will. Rietveld used his early training as a cabinetmaker

E-1027, Roquebrune-Cap-Martin, France, 1926–9: Eileen Gray.

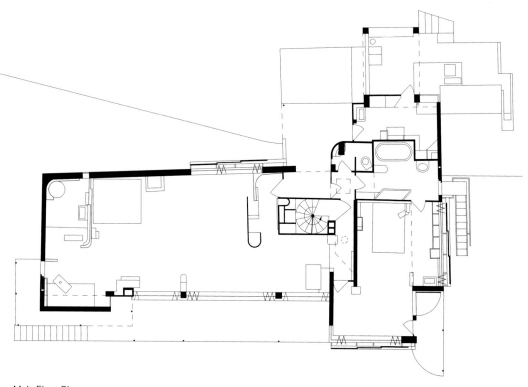

Main Floor Plan

Rietveld Schröder House,
Utrecht, the Netherlands, 1924–5:
Gerrit Rietveld.

to create a system of sliding and folding walls and surfaces that combined to divide the bathroom and bedrooms from the other spaces. Much of the furniture was built into this system, which accords with the De Stijl concepts of bold colour and spatial and formal definition. It is probable that Rietveld, initially at least, felt that this intellectual exploration of a new aesthetic movement was the area in which the house was innovative, rather than the creation of a changeable interior. This had, after all, resulted from his client's desire to live in a different way, rather than his own desire to experiment with new prototypical planning methods.[6] There is no doubt, however, that the present-day iconic status of the house stems as much from its famously flexible interior as it does from its modernist De Stijl image. By being so flexible, the Rietveld Schröder House seems to more fully achieve the stated ambitions of the modern movement houses that ostensibly heralded the free plan as the liberation of living space – in many cases this really meant putting the fixed walls into different configurations.

Begun in 1927, the Maison de Verre, designed by Pierre Chareau who was assisted by the Dutch architect Bernard Bijvoet, is the most enigmatic of these seminal European houses. Built on a notoriously difficult site replacing the lower two storeys of a four-storey eighteenth-century town house in the seventh arrondissement in Paris,

Rietveld Schröder House,
Utrecht, the Netherlands, 1924–5:
Gerrit Rietveld.

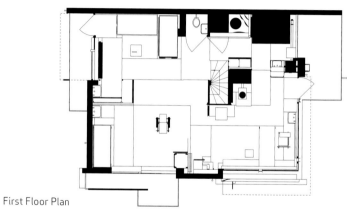

First Floor Plan

Flexible Home

the building was commissioned by Annie Bernheim and her physician husband, Jean Dalsace, and took five years to complete. Today, this building retains an astonishingly contemporary feel, not only for the dynamic, progressive interlocking space that flows from floor to floor, always defined by the luminous glass block walls that sandwich the dwelling in its remarkable location, but also for the almost unique consistency between the fittings, designed by Chareau (who was primarily a furniture and interior designer), and the building fabric. Glass, steel with expressive bolted or riveted joints, black slate, rubber and wood are used in fixed structural elements and flexible fittings – the walls slide, pivot and fold; wall cupboards rotate; and handrails, plant stands, tables and chairs take on the aesthetic of equipment rather than furnishings. The building also contains a dumbwaiter, a personnel lift and a unique retractable stairway that leads to the bedroom. Though essentially built as a bespoke object, a clear language of materials and dimensions can be perceived in the finished design. Consequently, the building expresses its constructed technology and the materials it is made of in a manner that has been hugely influential on contemporary architects (notably Richard Rogers) who design for similar effect.

The primary legacy of the modern movement house designs is the merging of space – undemarcated spaces that

Maison de Verre, Paris, France, 1927–31: Pierre Chareau.

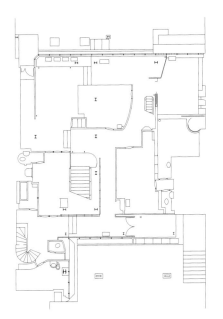

Ground Floor Plan

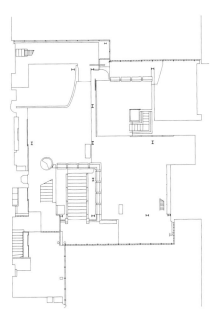

First Floor Plan

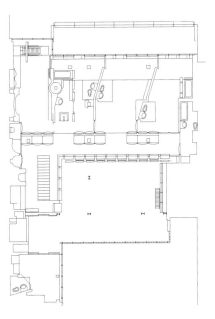

Second Floor Plan

are usually described as the free plan. However, almost as important must be the phenomenon of the disappearing wall. This is perhaps most evocatively expressed in Mies van der Rohe's Tugendhat House, built in Brno, Czech Republic in 1929–30. It was constructed at the same time as the Barcelona Pavilion in Spain (1928–9), which utilizes many of the trademark elements of Mies' early designs – open, continuous space (at least in the main living area); cruciform, chromed columns; vertical partitions of patterned stone and wood; and floor to ceiling glazed walls. The internal zones of the house are defined by the specially designed furniture – chairs, tables, sideboards and heavy velvet curtains that, when drawn, provide both visual and acoustic privacy. The glass wall is, however, the *tour de force*. Two of the large panes are fitted with a mechanism that enables them to be retracted fully into the floor below, transforming the room from a building to a pavilion and connecting it directly with the view over the city and across a wooded valley.

Mies' last house, built in Plano, Illinois, USA in 1950, is the Farnsworth House. Here, the idea of the floating glass pavilion with floor to ceiling glazing is carried to its ultimate extreme with completely glazed walls that create a mesmerizing, visual icon of floating architectural space. The only significant opening element is a pair of double doors at one end – though the walls of the Farnsworth House are

Tugendhat House, Brno, Czech Republic, 1929–30: Mies van der Rohe.

transparent they don't open up in any way, leading Mies' client to complain that the free space was 'actually very fixed'.[7]

Many other architects have since made use of the disappearing wall in rich and beautiful ways, for example Marcel Breuer, Craig Ellwood, Philip Johnson, Pierre Koenig, Oscar Niemeyer and Rudolph Schindler. Richard Neutra's 1946 house for the Kaufmann family (who had commissioned Frank Lloyd Wright's Falling Water ten years earlier) in Palm Springs used sliding glass screens to blur completely the edge between inside and outside living. Neutra also built a rooftop belvedere here with a different kind of moving wall, a set of vertical aluminium louvres that can be closed or opened to reveal the view and direct the desert breeze.

Though supposedly embodying the benefits of modern construction techniques, these iconic buildings were not designed as prototypical dwellings that might be made available to large sections of the population. However, Walter Gropius, influenced by his work with Peter Behrens at the AEG Company, did work on several projects for factory-built houses in the years before World War II, and exhibited a group of carefully designed prefabricated experimental houses at the 1927 *Weissenhofsiedlung* housing exhibition (directed by Mies van der Rohe) in Stuttgart. Although Le Corbusier's mass-housing design ideas were primarily focused on the multi-dwelling tower blocks of the Voisin Plan and the Ville

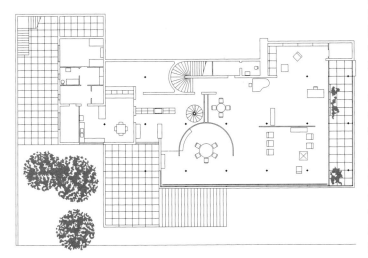

First Floor Plan

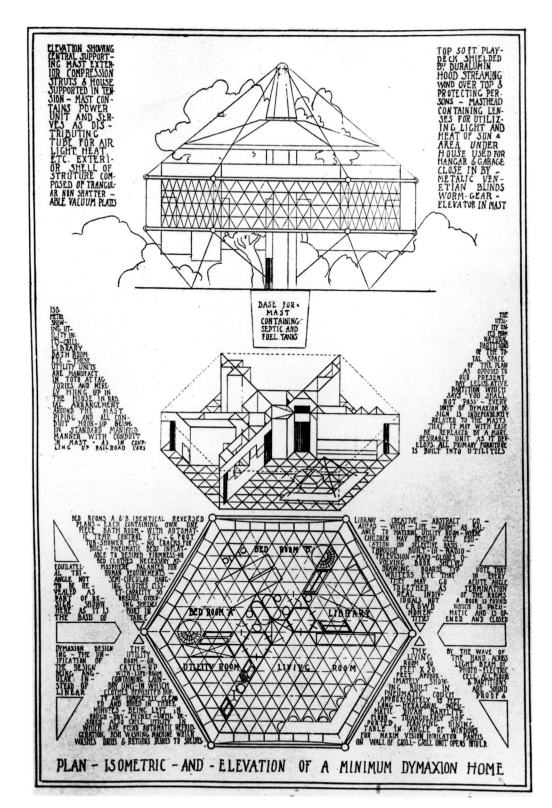

The illustration contains the following text:

Upper left: ELEVATION SHOWING CENTRAL SUPPORTING MAST EXTERIOR COMPRESSION STRUTS & HOUSE SUPPORTED IN TENSION - MAST CONTAINS POWER UNIT AND SERVES AS DISTRIBUTING TUBE FOR AIR LIGHT HEAT ETC - EXTERIOR SHELL OF STRUTURE COMPOSED OF TRANGULAR NON SHATTERABLE VACUUM PLATS

Upper right: TOP 50 FT. PLAYDECK SHIELDED BY DURALUMIN HOOD STREAMING WIND OVER TOP & PROTECTING PERSONS - MASTHEAD CONTAINING LENSES FOR UTILIZING LIGHT AND HEAT OF SUN & AREA UNDER HOUSE USED FOR HANGAR & GARAGE CLOSE IN BY METALIC VENETIAN BLINDS WORM-GEAR ELEVATOR IN MAST

Center label: BASE FOR MAST CONTAINING SEPTIC AND FUEL TANKS

Middle left: ISOMETRIC SHOWING UTILITY UNITS-GRILL LIBRARY BATH ROOM ETC - THESE UTILITY UNITS ARE MANUFACT IN TOTO AT FACTORIES AND MERELY HUNG UP IN THE HOUSE IN RADIAL ARRANGEMENT AROUND THE MAST PIPING AND ALL CONDUIT HOOK-UP BEING IN STANDARD MANIFOLD MANNER WITH CONDUIT IN MAST - AS IN COUPLING UP RAILROAD CARS

Middle right: THE UTILITY UNITS FORM NATURAL PARTITIONS OF THE TOTAL SPACE OF THE PLAN AS OPPOSED TO OUR PRESENT DAY LEGISLATIVE PARTITION WHICH SAYS YOU SHALL NOT PASS - EVERY UNIT OF DYMAXION DESIGN IS INDEPENDANTLY RELATED TO THE MASTS THAT IT MAY WITH EASE BE REPLACED BY A MORE DESIRABLE UNIT AS IT DEVELOPS. ALL PRIMARY FURNITURE IS BUILT INTO UTILITIES

Lower left: BED ROOMS A & B IDENTICAL REVERSED PLANS - EACH CONTAINING OWN ONE PIECE BATH ROOM WITH AUTOMATIC TEMP CONTROL ETC - 6 FOOT TUB-SHOWER ETC - NO CRACKS FOR BUGS - PNEUMATIC BEDS INFLATABLE TO DESIRED FIRMNESS-NO BED CLOTHES NECESSARY ATMOSPHERE BALANCED FOR HUMAN REQUIREMENTS

EQUILATERAL TRIANGLE NOT SEMI-CIRCULAR HANGING CLOTHES CLOSET-CAPACITY SO DRESSED-EVOLVING SHELVES BUILT IN TABLE

NOT TO BE REVEALED AS PART OF DESIGN SHOWN HERE AS IT IS THE BASIS OF

DYMAXION DESIGNING - THE UNIFICATION OF THE DESIGN BEING ANGULAR INSTEAD OF LINEAR

THE UTILITY ROOM OR CATCH-UP UNIT WITH LIFE-LONG CONTAINING LAUNDRY UNIT IN WHICH CLOTHES DEPOSITED DIRTY ARE COMPLETELY CLEANED AND DRIED IN THREE MINUTES - BEING LEFT IN POUCH-DRY-POCKET-UNTIL DESIRED AND GRILL UTILITY IN WHICH ARE FOUND AUTOMATIC REFRIGERATION, DISH WASHING MACHINE WHICH WASHES DRIES & RETURNS DISHES TO SHELVES

Lower right: LIBRARY - CREATIVE - ABSTRACT - GO AHEAD WITH - LIFE - ROOM AS BALANCE TO MATERIAL UTILITY ROOM - CHILDREN MAY DEVELOP SELF EDUCATION ON SELECTIVE BASIS THROUGH BUILT-IN RADIO TELEVISION-MAPS-GLOBES-REVOLVING BOOK SHELVES DRAWING BOARDS TYPEWRITERS ETC - ETC

NOTE THAT ACUTE ANGLE IN EVERY REAL INDIVIDUALS NOT CROWD NONENTITIES

THEY MAY GO TOGETHER AS TERMINATION OF THE ROOMS A FLOOR IS FOUND WHICH IS PNEUMATIC AND IS OPENED AND CLOSED

THE LIVING ROOM 40 FEET X 20 FEET APPROXIMATELY SHOWING BUILT IN PNEUMATIC COUCH APPROXIMATELY 15 FEET LONG - HEXAGONAL PNEUMATIC DIVAN BAKELITE FLOOR TRIANGULARLY SUPPORTED HANGING DINING TABLE IN ANGLE OF WINDOWS FOR MAXIM VISION INDICATOR PANELS ON WALL OF GRILL-GRILL UNIT OPENS INTO L.R.

BY THE WAVE OF THE HAND ACROSS LIGHT BEAM OF PHOTO-ELECTRIC CELL ALL FLOORS & PARTITIONS ARE SOUND PROOF

Room labels: BED ROOM B, BED ROOM A, LIBRARY, UTILITY ROOM, LIVING ROOM

Bottom title: PLAN - ISOMETRIC - AND - ELEVATION OF A MINIMUM DYMAXION HOME

Dymaxion House, Chicago, USA, 1929: Buckminster Fuller.

Radieuse, he also designed a small production housing project during this period, which was not, however, very successful.[8]

The exploration of industrial techniques in housing design was not confined to Europe. Prefabrication building techniques were recognized not just as a way to introduce the industrial aesthetic, but also to improve quality and speed of construction. The main potential to improve flexibility was in the capacity to make factory-based manufacture remote from the site, and the ability of modularization to deliver varied layouts with the same components. In 1931 Albert Frey, a Swiss architect who had worked in Le Corbusier's office on the Villa Savoye project, designed and built the Aluminaire House in collaboration with Lawrence Kocher, managing editor of the New York-based journal *Architectural Record*. The house was initially built as the centrepiece of the Allied Arts and Building Products Exhibition in New York City, though it was then relocated to Long Island for permanent erection. The building had many innovative construction techniques, not least its prefabrication enabling it to be erected in just ten days and disassembled in six. Made with an aluminium and steel frame and clad in profiled aluminium panels, it was created to a very restricted floor plan in order to fit into the space it was allocated at the exhibition. Frey designed many multiple-use furnishings – beds suspended from cables, translucent room partitions that folded away to maximize the feeling of space, and a table that expanded out from the wall with a top that rolled out on a cylinder. Easily stored, inflatable furniture was also designed for the house, but never actually made.

The problem with the prototypical, mass-produced house design at this time was finding the funding that was needed to bring it into production. Traditional building companies and trade unions fought against the ideas, fearing massive unemployment in their industries if the designers achieved what they predicted.[9]

Though it only ever existed in prototype form, Buckminster Fuller's Dymaxion House (1929) is certainly the most famous example of a house design that focused on mass-production to achieve a high-quality, individual dwelling environment for large numbers of people at affordable cost. The term Dymaxion, which Fuller used to describe many of his inventions, was coined by the promotions manager of the Marshall Field's store in Chicago where, in 1929, Fuller lectured and exhibited a model of the 4D house that he had designed. The building had little to do with the current architectural styles or theories of the time and took its sole manifesto to be the comfort and protection of its occupiers by using the latest technology, much of which was only just being realized. Fuller's enthusiastic lectures described a factory-built building, transported to site and erected in days.

Flexible Home

It was earthquake, flood and tornado proof, air-conditioned, fully fitted with furnishings and components, such as radio, television (which had just been exhibited for the first time that year), typewriter and calculating machine. The house was self-contained with its own power generator, sewage disposal and an amphibian airplane-automobile transport unit. The re-named Dymaxion House had immense media coverage, much of it favourable. However, the burgeoning Depression made construction impossible.

By 1945, as World War II came to an end, the Beech Aircraft Company was seeking a new manufacturing role and enlisted Fuller to collaborate on the design of a viable version of the Dymaxion House. Although the image of this later building was somewhat different, many of Fuller's original labour-saving, environmental and flexible design ideas remained. Once more his design (now a full-size prototype) received generally favourable publicity. All the components of the new house could be fitted into a 4.8 x 1.3 metre (15.8 x 4.3 foot) cylindrical shipping container, and eight of these tubes could be carried on a single railway truck. The house could be erected in 200 hours, which equated to approximately two working days by a crew of 16 trained people.[10] By 1946, 37,000 unsolicited orders had been taken for the product, predicted to be in production at a price of $6,500 for each of the 250,000 units made per year.

The Wichita House, prototyped by the Beech Aircraft Company, Kansas, USA, 1945: Buckminster Fuller.

But production never went ahead. Beech executives said that Fuller refused to relinquish the design control for manufacturing to commence, and continued to make myriad detailed changes until they were forced to shelve the project. Fuller said that the industry was not ready for such a product, as there was no way to ship or install the building, and he felt it would not be honest to sell something he knew he could not deliver.[11]

The USA had suffered from five years of under-investment in building, due to the war effort, which had resulted in a large shortfall in new houses and Fuller's Dymaxion House was intended to fulfil that need. In the UK, however, the need was even more desperate as bombing had also destroyed 400,000 homes. The Temporary Housing Programme was instigated by the government as the end of the war seemed in sight to supply as many houses as they could as quickly as possible and to make use of redundant armament factories to do it. In this situation, resistance from the traditional building industries was irrelevant and experimentation in construction methods and materials was actively encouraged – standardization became the key to speed, economy and flexibility.

There were four main house-production systems: the Arcon; the AIROH; the Uni-Seco; and the Tarran, all similar in layout though differing in construction materials and methods. Despite an environment of reduced labour availability and materials restrictions, these systems produced over 130,000 new homes in the five years after the war ended. The AIROH Aluminium Bungalow, made by aircraft manufacturers Bristol, was the most technically impressive and the most numerous (54,500 were produced). Perhaps by accident, the form of these simply planned buildings – independent two-bedroom cottages with indoor bathroom, fitted kitchen and their own small garden space – allowed their inhabitants to adapt their new homes to their own needs. The 'pre-fabs', as they were affectionately known, were immensely popular. They provided a direct link with the perfect home (at least in England) of a traditional cottage, but at the same time were simple, modern buildings that allowed their inhabitants, after a period of extreme deprivation and uncertainty, to establish a new home for themselves and even to personalize it by furnishing, decorating and gardening. The only comparable undertaking in the US was the government funded, though commercially produced, Lustron Home. However, after consuming $40 million over three years with only 2,500 homes to show for it, the company was closed down.

US industry did eventually create a viable prefabricated house – the mobile home. They were 'mobile' primarily in the sense that they could be delivered to almost

The AIROH (Aircraft Industry Research Organisation on Housing) Aluminium Bungalow production line at the Weston-super-Mare factory of Bristol Co., 1946. Constructed of riveted aluminium sheets, the building was delivered to site in prefabricated volumetric units complete with wiring, fitted kitchens and bathrooms.

'Adobe' Mobile Homes, Arizona, USA. Prefabricated, light-weight, easily transportable factory-made buildings that can be 'adapted' to the local 'style'.

any site with ease – only a small percentage are ever relocated. Instead of relying on sophisticated manufacturing techniques and comparatively expensive materials, these affordable, factory-built buildings used simple timber framing and readily available, cheap and conventional materials to provide ready-built homes across the country. This was the product of a diverse industry with many separate companies spread throughout the country to meet regional needs.

From the beginnings in the 1930s and 1940s to the present day, mobile home manufacturers have been able to respond to the needs of their clients and have steadily increased both the variety and quality of their product, changing its name in the process to 'manufactured housing' in a bid to sidestep the prejudice that is sometimes associated with these affordable buildings. These houses are now often built to higher standards than other 'in-situ' constructed buildings in the USA because they take advantage of repetitive details that are assembled in conducive factory conditions. Plans are very flexible, due to the nature of the framed construction method, and the completed buildings come with a wide range of already fitted conveniences, finishes and appliances and in an almost infinite range of 'styles' from Georgian to 'adobe'. More than a quarter of all new homes delivered in North America are provided by the manufactured housing industry and it is interesting to note

that architects are now prepared to take this strategy seriously, with a network of 'designerly' versions that are marketed via the Internet.[12]

From the 1950s onwards, industrial building techniques on a much larger scale began to replace the pre-fabs and millions of older houses in cities around the world: concrete tower blocks; deck dwellings; houses built within large structures, each containing dozens if not hundreds of homes. In the UK these buildings have one similarity with the separate dwellings provided under the Temporary Housing Programme – the plan layouts remained conventional and the focus was on delivering modern conveniences, such as indoor bathrooms and fitted kitchens, and as many new houses as quickly and as cheaply as possible. In many ways mass industrial techniques adopted around the world after World War II delivered what the modernists of the pre-war period predicted – housing for everyone to set standards. What it also delivered was dispossession of the notion of home by reducing their built form to dwellings that consisted of an inflexible minimum space. Because of urban planning, design and construction it was also almost impossible for the inhabitants to appropriate these spaces.

The idea of utilizing industrial techniques to make individual houses remained a particular preoccupation of the post-war years, especially in the USA. In 1945, the Museum

of Modern Art in New York organized the exhibition, *Tomorrow's Small House*, which showed full-size examples of buildings designed by many notable architects of the day, including Philip Johnson, Frank Lloyd Wright, George Fred Keck and Carl Koch. All of these buildings were, to a greater or lesser degree, intended to utilize prefabrication techniques. Also in 1945, John Entenza began a programme of Case Study Houses for the magazine, *Arts & Architecture*. Case Study House #8, built in 1948 by Charles and Ray Eames for themselves and aided by Eero Saarinen, was undoubtedly the most influential of these buildings. It was an inhabited, over-sized jewellery box made from industrial, off-the-shelf components intended to contain the Eames' collection of craft and art objects and to facilitate their own informal lifestyle. Each space flowed into the next – in the case of the link between house and studio across an external courtyard. Art objects, rugs, furnishings and plants were scattered around the floor surfaces, attached to walls and ceilings, and suspended in space. The Eames subsequently designed a modular toy house, manufactured by Revell, which seemed to duplicate the enjoyable, relaxed atmosphere that they had created for their own home.

Throughout the twentieth century there has been a fascination with the search for the 'ideal' home, and many of these designs have focused on flexibility and adaptability as

Eames House (Case Study House
#8), Santa Monica, 1948: Charles
and Ray Eames with Eero Saarinen.

Plug-In City, 1964: Peter Cook,
Archigram.

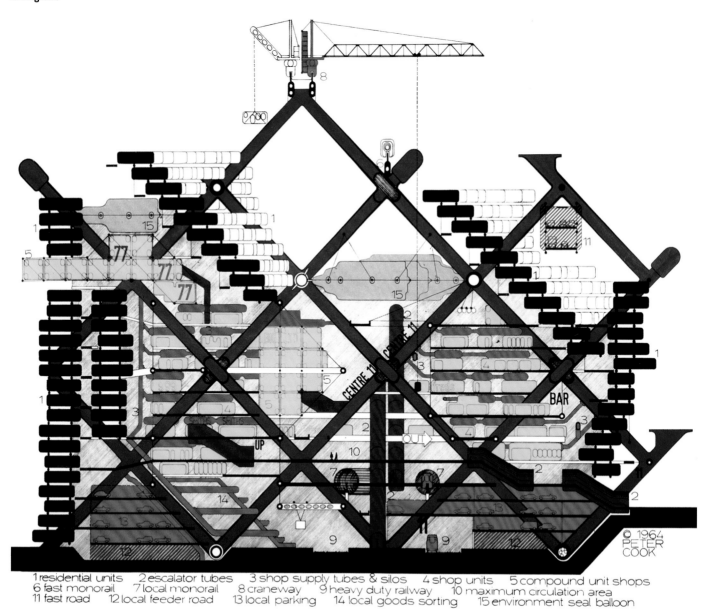

1 residential units   2 escalator tubes   3 shop supply tubes & silos   4 shop units   5 compound unit shops
6 fast monorail   7 local monorail   8 craneway   9 heavy duty railway   10 maximum circulation area
11 fast road   12 local feeder road   13 local parking   14 local goods sorting   15 environment seal balloon

Flexible Home

a key innovative element. However, to try to predict the future of the house is also to predict the social and cultural future – how will we live and what will we need or aspire to? There have been countless prototypical 'homes of the future' that regularly create great interest among the design professions and public alike. The key to why these experimental designs, many very practical and tuned into perceived needs, have not passed beyond the prototype stage is indicated by the nature of the sponsor – often those who only make or sell the usual, the typical or the conventional product.

Buckminster Fuller's Dymaxion House was exhibited as a publicity stunt in 1929 to bring in customers to see the latest range of imported French furniture at Marshall Field's Chicago department store. Frederick Kiesler's Space House, an organic shell-like structure that allowed the interior to be a continuous, flowing volume with varied floor levels and space that was delineated by movable partitions, was created for the Modernage Furniture Company, New York in 1933. Alison and Peter Smithson's 1956 design for the House of the Future used organic, interlocking spaces made of plastic and incorporating built-in cooking, washing and entertainment equipment. It was sponsored by and located at the *Daily Mail Ideal Home Exhibition* in London, an established commercial showcase for house builders and DIY enthusiasts. Despite the

very real opportunities they offered, these exhibits were primarily regarded by the sponsors as exciting crowd teasers and perceived by the exhibit visitors as present-day entertainment, rather than future reality.

There is no doubt, however, that prototypical house designs have influenced the development of architectural form through the issues that they have explored and communicated to subsequent designers. Experimental design also influences the mainstream and eventually many ideas and concepts, once considered stimulating and exciting though impractical, suddenly appear realizable. The 1960s saw a major outpouring of experimental architectural design, linked to the counter-culture that had permeated society in reaction to rampant commercialism, the tensions of the Cold War and the dreary monotony of most new urban development. Apparently simultaneously, an assortment of young, avant-garde groups emerged around the world: Ant Farm and EAT (Experiments in Art and Architecture) in the USA; Archizoom, UFO and Superstudio in Italy; Coop Himmelblau, Haus-Rucker-Co. and Missing Link in Austria; Utopie in France; the Metabolists in Japan; and Archigram in the UK. Most of these groups set out to challenge the conventional view of architecture. In particular they experimented with new materials and techniques from other industries to suggest unconventional environments, some of

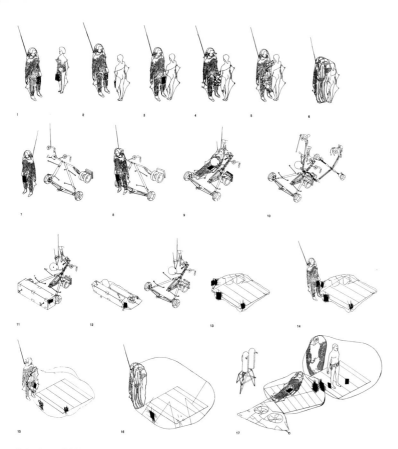

Suitaloon, 1968: Michael Webb, Archigram.

which were intended to be completely new spatial experiences for meditation, mind-expanding or simple enjoyment. Others were seen as replacements for recognizable building types, such as the house. All, however, were intended to be provocative.

Archigram's work was perhaps the most widely publicized, primarily because the group's intention was to communicate ideas rather than to philosophize. Indeed, many of Archigram's ideas have subsequently been explored in reality, though by others rather than the group's original members. Plug-In City, a concept by Peter Cook and published in 1964, was one of several projects that dealt with the idea of prefabricated homes assembled into dense fluctuating urban patterns. Other projects on the same theme were Capsule Homes by Warren Chalk (1964) and Gasket Homes by Warren Chalk and Ron Herron (1965).[13]

The Japanese Metabolist group emerged simultaneously with Archigram, but because of Japan's 'economic miracle' of rapid commercial growth at the time they were able to build at least some of their projects, including Kisho Kurokawa's Nakagin Capsule Tower, Tokyo (1972), which at least partly realized the plug-in concept. The capsule hotel, found across Japan in dedicated buildings or occupying just a few floors of a multi-purpose structure, can also be traced back to Archigram roots. The group's ideas

Nakagin Capsule Tower, Tokyo, Japan, 1972: Kisho Kurokawa.

about the one-off dwelling were also stimulating. In 1966, inspired by NASA's space suits and survival capsules, Michael Webb created the Cushicle, a portable, one-person environment suit that enabled the individual to travel anywhere in fully serviced comfort. Webb's Suitaloon (1968) developed this concept further with a design for a pneumatic home, worn like a suit and inflated when required. It could also be attached to optional extras, such as an engine and wheels to convert it into a personal vehicle. The twenty-first-century version of the Suitaloon is the Bio-Shelter from Polaris International, a pressurized, air-filtered tent that is intended to offer a home and protection against germ warfare. It is remarkably similar in appearance to Webb's design, though of course instead of lifestyle expanding its effect is lifestyle restricting.

Pneumatic structures used to create inflatable living spaces were particularly popular with these experimental groups as they made use of a burgeoning technology that possessed powerful associated imagery – instant architecture that was flexible and organic. In 1967, Jean-Paul Jungmann designed the Dyodon, an experimental pneumatic dwelling made from inflatable panels that formed a multi-storey space with integral inflatable furniture. Coop Himmelblau created the Villa Rosa in the following year. This was a pneumatic living environment that could be carried in a

Micro Compact Home, Germany, 2004:
Horden Cherry Lee Architects and
Haack and Hoepfner Architects.

suitcase, had a built-in inflatable bed and could be connected
to other spaces for group living or entertainment. After the
1960s, experimental architecture seemed to shift from being
a radical movement, intent on challenging the establishment,
to something that designers did to get their work noticed
prior to winning a big commission. However, there were still
some notable ideas that captured imaginations, if not
potential clients.

London-based architects Amanda Levette and
Jan Kaplicky are principals of Future Systems, which has
designed a range of technologically inspired, hypothetical
dwellings. This began in 1975 with Cabin 380, a building
design that utilizes vehicle imagery and technology to
create a minimal mobile house that can be located
anywhere. Sharing the seductive communication technique
of Archigram, but far more production focused in their
approach to design, Future Systems created a family of
developing house designs over the next 15 years, while
also carrying out commissioned work for NASA involving
accommodation in space. Though many designers have
explored the concept of sophisticated mobile, technological
dwellings that can be dropped into any environment, few
have been realized. Architect Richard Horden, however, has
regularly prototyped small, technology-based shelters. The
Skihaus is an airliftable building that serves as an alpine

Skihaus, Switzerland, 1990–2005:
Richard Horden.

Airstream trailer – Excella model of
the classic 'silver bullet', from 1979.

shelter for two people. It is built around the design restraint
of the weight of a cow, the heaviest object the Swiss Alps
mountain rescue helicopters can carry. Ten years after its
first deployment, the Skihaus is still being airlifted to new
locations. Horden has gone on to create other minimal mobile
shelters including the Micro Compact Home at Technische
Universität München with Horden Cherry Lee Architects and
Haack and Hoepfner Architects, a mass-produced, stackable
living unit aimed at providing affordable accommodation
for students and other single city-centre dwellers.

The most commonly realized movable dwelling is the
caravan or trailer home. Initially built as special one-off
designs for rich travellers, the archetypal precedent for the
sophisticated mobile caravan is the Airstream 'silver bullet'
trailer. Though continuously developed since its introduction
in 1935, its image has not changed – an evocative shining
aerodynamic bubble, a form that has persisted for good
practical reasons, being easy to maintain and light and
stable for good towing. Though the interior of the Airstream
has always been ingenious and practical, it has not typically
matched the exterior in terms of design quality. The latest
model, a remake of the classic Bambi design, has been
reinvented by the design team iNSIDEdesign, to create a
practical yet aesthetic environment in a smaller vehicle
suitable for narrower roads than the North American highways.

Buckminster Fuller was no doubt aware of the precedent of the camper trailer when he designed the Mechanical Wing (1940), a towable facility that contained washing, cooking and heating services that could be plugged into any simple shelter.[14] Most modern camper trailers use a number of devices to increase space once they have arrived at their location, such as rising roofs and push-out rooms. Perhaps the simplest system is a roll-up awning that can extend from the side of the trailer to make a covered space that forms an external 'living' room. Netherlands architect Eduard Böhtlingk's Markies (meaning 'awning' in Dutch) camper trailer uses this strategy, but in a sophisticated manner. Much like Fuller's Mechanical Wing, the simple trailer form contains all the domestic servicing facilities, but once the unit arrives at its destination the walls fold down to make floors and the new space is enclosed by a concertina-like membrane structure that is transparent on the living side of the dwelling and translucent on the sleeping side. Beds, chairs and tables fold down from the central compartment to create a new space for circulation. The transformation from anonymous trailer to romantic residence is a large part of the attraction.

Maartje Lammers and Boris Zeisser, principals of Rotterdam-based 24H Architecture, have converted an eighteenth-century fisherman's cottage at Ové Glas, in Sweden's Glaskogen nature reserve, into a seasonal

Markies, the Netherlands, 1985–95:
Eduard Böhtlingk.

Flexible Home

residence. Because of restrictions on the size of the developments allowed in the area, and also their desire to make a building that changed from winter to summer use, 24H Architecture have created a transformable design in which the main living space has an entire room section that opens up like a drawer. Using a system of pulleys and a steel frame mounted on roller bearings, the structure can be easily changed by just one person. As it extends to overhang a stream, running adjacent to the site, it reveals the building's main window, which is oriented towards the water. The organic 'growing' building is clad externally in red cedar shingles and internally with silver birch laths and draped in reindeer skins. Lighting is provided by solar power and heating by a log stove.

The Markies and the Ové Glas House were realized after great effort and determination, but numerous other experimental residential projects, apparently even more ambitious than these, have also been proposed. Their proliferation is fuelled by the belief that it is now truly possible to challenge not only what a house needs to be, but also how the idea of a house relates to the idea of architecture in general. Most remain conceptual designs, made more understandable and more challenging by the immediacy of contemporary computer-based design and presentation techniques. It is now easier to appreciate a

potential design through animated, real-time walk-through than it was by just looking at Fuller's acetate and cardboard model of his Dymaxion House. A few contemporary designs do make it through to the prototype stage and begin the real test of combining materials, structure and construction into a workable, environmentally comfortable facility. The problems involved in making experimental architecture both workable and affordable are often underestimated by designers, and this struggle is, understandably, most often not overcome. Even if such experimental, one-off designs could be built, it is questionable whether or not they can fundamentally change mainstream housing design. This is because, although the one-off house is undoubtedly an essential tool in delivering architectural innovation, it is not a solution to which most people can aspire.

Making *housing* as opposed to *a house* has a fundamentally different agenda from one-off designs and involves very different problems for the designer who wishes to provide adaptability for the occupants. The one-off house, whether it is created by a well-known architect, espousing a set of ideas and criteria besides those set by the client, or by an individual working alone or with professionals to make something very personal, is a comparatively high-profile, though small, part of total housing provision. Far more dwellings are made as part of collective housing projects,

Ové Glas House, Sweden, 2004: 24H.
Floor plans of main living space in
closed and extended states.

sponsored from public funds or commercial, profit-motivated
projects, in buildings where the inhabitants have had very
little, if any, contact with the designer. The design of a
one-off house, either for a client or as an experiment, is
completely different from designing mass housing, either
public or private. The former is often based on first-hand
knowledge and clearly voiced desires and concerns, and the
latter is based on speculative, even fictitious, assumptions,
even though there may be a 'real' client in the form of a
developer. If we examine just one factor in the equation, the
nature of the family, it is easy to see that there is an amazing
plurality that has to be dealt with in terms of balance
between children, adults and the elderly. It might easily be
assumed that the children are involved in education, but
which of the adults is employed, involved in childcare or
further education? A household in which the father looks
after the child, the mother works and the grandmother
attends university is manifestly possible. Flexibility in the
design of collective housing is essential if designers wish
to provide for the dichotomy of lifestyles of the occupants.

It is possible to define the different typologies of
collective housing flexibility in an expanding hierarchy.
Firstly, flexibility must be established prior to occupation
as a way of allowing different variations within the same
architectural form. Secondly, there must be the flexibility

to make possible the potential for future change. This latter type of flexible design has also been further subdivided by Gustau Gili Galfetti into three types: 'mobility' allows for the rapid change of spaces on a virtually instantaneous basis, allowing for day-to-day reconfiguration; 'evolution' describes a built-in capacity for long-term modification to the basic layout over a period of years; 'elasticity' concerns the expansion or contraction of the habitable space.[15]

The careful thought that is necessary to deal with all these possibilities is far more likely to be applied in the case of well-funded public projects, as the majority of commercial mass-house-building companies are unwilling to spend their profit margin on the design of such complex flexible housing. It would also, undoubtedly, lead to construction and planning innovations that would price their product above those of their competitors. It is only in the relatively expensive niche markets, such as city-centre apartments, where some builders are now forced to keep pace with their clients whose aspirations have changed towards houses that are unfettered by clichés. The vast majority perceive that their remit is to give the customer what they want, though often what this amounts to is what the builder gives them – in many cases this means bland, nostalgic imitations of the past placed in arbitrary juxtapositions and forming meaningless 'non-places'. These 'trans-cultural' buildings

WoZoCo elderly persons' housing, Amsterdam, the Netherlands, 1999: MVRDV.
An immense sense of place and individuality is provided by this radical solution in a residential type that tends usually to be extremely conservative.

are intended for 'occupation' by the purchase of commercially available mass-culture products.[16]

Though people are of course entitled to have any sort of home they desire, such buildings are ultimately not their own choice at all. They are subversively imposed through intensive marketing by mass-consumer organizations that seek to homogenize society for the commercial advantage this affords them. Large groups of people automatically consuming the same goods without question makes for easy, repetitive, continuous sales strategies for the large, international, commercial conglomerates. Such 'homes', by their very nature, cannot afford to reflect the important influences of location, site and the particular desires of the individual occupant. This sort of mass building detracts not only from the freedom of the occupant, but also, by its devastating abandonment of regional context and the rapid sprawl that absorbs green space and farmland, chokes the towns and villages it swallows. As Dutch architects/planners MVRDV have advocated in their FARMAX proposals and built projects, it is far better to build densely in cities with contemporary, adaptable patterns, and if it is necessary to build in rural environments to do so lightly, with low impact.[17]

Crossover between the realms of high-cost dwelling design and mass housing does occur, however, and the experience gained working on one-off projects for relatively

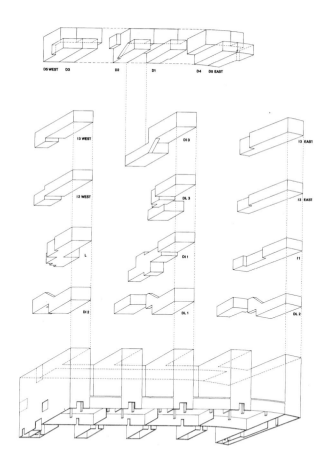

Fukuoka Housing, Fukuoka, Japan, 1989–91: Steven Holl.
Diagram integrating the different interlocking apartments situated within each block.

wealthy clients can be applied to collective housing. From 1983, architect Steven Holl began to experiment with the concept of 'hinged space', particularly in housing. 'Hinged space' is generated by moving walls that 'participate' with their inhabitants in the creation of interactive environments. By pushing, pulling and physically manipulating these separators and surfaces, people can reorder their home to their liking, and so the space they have becomes contingent on the space they need. Holl's initial projects were in New York City's Manhattan apartments (the Cohen, X-Y-Z, and Theo-logical) where space is always at a premium. However, a more extensive exploration of the possibilities of domestic hinged space came in 1989 with the Fukuoka Housing project in Japan. Holl's initial presentation to the client was for a range of apartments, some of which incorporated the hinged space concept and some of which contained conventional fixed walls. The client's response was to insist that all the apartments utilize the hinged-space concept. The project consists of five buildings organized around four water courts. The buildings contain 28 apartments in total, each of which is different, which incorporate alternative movable walls, corners and surfaces that fold and rotate depending on the needs of the occupant. The apartments are indeterminate and incomplete rather than autonomous and fixed and the occupants can manipulate the space on a daily basis, responding to the patterns of sleeping, eating, work and leisure. They can also react to seasonal needs, creating a feeling of enclosure and protection in a winter storm and letting light flood the entire space on a spring day.

Though also situated in Japan, NEXT21 is a very different attempt to build flexibility into multi-family housing and to explore the best strategies for constructing future urban dwellings. Begun in 1993 and sponsored by Osaka Gas Co. Ltd, it is an experimental building that is intended to try out different environmental, energy and amenities strategies over the long-term. The project began with discussions between building-industry specialists and environmentalists to ascertain what critical problems their respective areas faced. The resulting brief was to design an urban apartment building that could accept radical changes in servicing and dwelling layouts with minimal disruption so it could act as a test-bed for innovative design. The building uses a two-stage system to meet the aims of the research team and individual residents' needs or lifestyles. A reinforced concrete structural frame forms the first stage, which is a long-term, relatively fixed construction. Interiors are the second stage and were designed separately. Four of the 18 dwellings were designed together with residents and, as this is an experimental platform, the remaining apartments consist of different, enhanced living environments proposed by the design team.

Fukuoka Housing, Fukuoka, Japan, 1991: Steven Holl.

Many of the building's components are standardized, including external cladding, so that they can be easily replaced or relocated if required. Varied dwelling layouts can then be fitted within this flexible system, including a work home, a child-friendly home and a quiet home. A range of new domestic technology is currently under test in the project, including a refuse compacter and transporter, centrally heated tatami mats and an automatic bath washer. Great care was taken with materials so that they did not include solvents, such as formaldehyde found in plywood and chipboard, and only nails were used for fixing to avoid the use of glue solvents. The building incorporates an extremely flexible, concealed service layout that allows a range of advanced energy-conscious systems to be installed and monitored during actual use by the residents. Changes can be made to the system as required not only to respond to the residents' comments and requests, but also so that new service systems that require testing can be installed and different strategies explored.

It can be appreciated from this examination of the flexible home that the success of domestic architecture is directly connected to its flexibility. The design of contemporary housing is not something that can be reduced to a specific set of rigid rules to provide a universal model. Indeed, some projects designed in this way, although carried out with great care, can now be labelled as 'obstructive residential environments' that restrict individuals' ability to use their new homes properly.[18] Homes require flexibility to allow for adaptation by the resident over time. Even if they have been designed specifically for someone, people and their circumstances change and even a carefully tailored suit can still grow too tight and go out of style in time. Enabling people to use their homes in their own individual way and to alter their environment to their own requirements not only allows them to transform a building from an anonymous space into a specific 'place', but it also provides the flexibility to change with circumstances.

NEXT21, Osaka, Japan, 1993–4: Yositika Utida, SHU-KO-SHA architects.

1 Jonathan Bell in the introduction to 'The Transformable House', *Architectural Design*, profile no.146, vol.70, no.4, 2000, p.5.
2 As Beatriz Colomina succinctly states in her essay 'The Media House': 'The house is the best advertisement for architecture.' See Mechtild Stuhlmacher and Rien Korteknie (eds.), *The City of Small Things*, Rotterdam, 2001, p.105.
3 Mies van der Rohe is reputed to have said that in relation to the development of the Modern Movement, 'Wright saved us fifty years.' See Jonathan Lipman, 'The Art and Craft of the Machine: An Overview of the Work of Frank Lloyd Wright' in *Frank Lloyd Wright Retrospective*, exh. cat., Tokyo, 1991, p.28.
4 The Van der Leeuw House is examined in Neil Jackson, *The Modern Steel House*, London, 1996, pp.19–24.
5 Eileen Gray and Jean Badovici, 'Description' [of E-1027], *L'Architecture Vivante*, Winter 1929, p.23, as quoted in Sarah Whiting, 'Voices Between the Lines: Talking in the Gray Zone' in Caroline Constant and Wilfred Wang (eds.), *Eileen Gray: An Architecture for All Senses*, Berlin, Frankfurt-am-Main and Cambridge, Mass., 1996, pp.72–83.
6 See Catherine Croft, 'Movement and Myth: The Schröder House and Transformable Living' in 'The Transformable House', *Architectural Design*, profile no.146, vol.70, no.4, 2000, pp.10–15.
7 See Ken Tadashi Oshima and Toshiko Kiroshita, *A&U Visions of the Real: Modern Houses in the 20th Century II*, Tokyo, 2000, p.12. A small window could also be opened in the sleeping area.
8 See Colin St John Wilson, *The Other Tradition of Modern Architecture: The Uncompleted Project*, London, 1995. In 1929, Le Corbusier also realized a Parisian Salvation Army floating shelter for 160 homeless residents that was built on a reinforced concrete barge.
9 For an examination of the inter-war innovative US house design prototypes see H. Ward Jandl, *Yesterday's Houses of Tomorrow: Innovative American Homes 1850–1950*, Washington, DC, 1991.
10 The prototype house could also be dismantled for relocation.
11 For a detailed examination of Fuller's work see Joachim Krausse and Claud Lichtenstein, *Your Private Sky: R. Buckminster Fuller, Art of Design Science/Your Private Sky: Discourse*, Baden, 1999.
12 Modular Modern is a New York-based organization that markets contemporary factory-built homes designed by leading practices on a global basis. Projects by Jones Partners, Adam Kalkin, and Cartwright Pickard are among those featured.
13 See Peter Cook (ed.), *Archigram*, London, 1972.
14 In particular the Dymaxion Deployment Unit, a simple building developed from the commercially manufactured Butler grain bin that was another precursor of the Beech-made Dymaxion House.
15 See Gustau Gili Galfetti, *Model Apartments: Experimental Domestic Cells*, Barcelona, 1997, p.13.
16 See Manuel Gausa, 'Reversible Habitat (other ways of housing)' in *Archilab 2001*, Orléans, 2001, p.37.
17 MVRDV, as well as creating buildings that radically uphold this view, notably WoZoCo elderly persons' housing, Amsterdam (1999) and 3D – Tuin (3D – Tower) office and apartment block, Hengelo (2001), have also created two publications, *FARMAX* (1998) and *Datascape* (1999), to communicate this philosophy.
18 See Antje Flade, 'Psychological Considerations of Dwelling' in Mathias Schwartz-Clauss (ed.), *Living in Motion: Design and Architecture for Flexible Dwelling*, Weil-am-Rhein, 2002, pp.220–37.

Flexible Community

Architecture that is able to create a sense of place is just as important in non-domestic building as it is in the home. The practical advantages of adaptability in many aspects of building provision are also important. Where this has been recognized by clients, designers and builders, remarkable precedents for flexible architecture have resulted.

Stata Center, Cambridge, Mass., USA, 2005: Frank Gehry.

The pressure for responsive change in the contemporary built environment is recognized in the principles adopted by the advocates of the design policy known as Open Building, which was first articulated as a design strategy by John Habraken in the early 1960s.[1] Habraken believed that architecture required a new set of design principles that actively supported the probability of change. He proposed that buildings should consist of serviced frameworks to which rooms and spaces could be added in a form directly influenced by experience and practice. One of the key principles of Open Building is the realization that the built environment is the result of collaboration between many people with many different types of skills, and that these should be harnessed in order to create appropriate solutions. It also supports the concept that a new design is not finite at the point of delivery to the client, but is part of an ongoing, continuous process of use, adaptation and evolution under the influence of users and inhabitants. A key Open Building concept is that environmental design operates at a number of related, but distinct, levels of complexity ranging from the city to the individual room. In this scenario flexible architecture is most significant at the level of the building and the levels immediately subordinate to that, such as a suite of offices within an administration building or an individual room within the office. However, in addition the impact of architecture extends to higher levels particularly at the neighbourhood level, but also, on occasion, at the city level. Wherever built form is to be designed, and whatever the scale of the intervention, flexibility is therefore a key consideration.

Nevertheless, there are some places, established by architectural form, that have greater importance than others because they impact more significantly on the way society operates. Human beings are individuals but humanity evolves and develops because of its society. Society exists through the collaboration of individuals sharing skills and resources. Continued progress in society occurs when new ways of working together are found. Therefore, perhaps the most important architectural spaces outside the home are the places that have been established where meetings between individuals occur. Their importance is emphasized by the fact that they are the most ubiquitous architectural space and are found in every kind of urban and rural environment, and in every type of building. Despite this, it is extremely hard to define any specific character for the optimum meeting space – is it a classroom, convention centre, courtroom or a nightclub?

The meeting place is the quintessential flexible space. It must allow for the needs of a range of different users, and in many cases the types and scale of activities vary greatly. The earliest meeting spaces were open-air, sometimes in spaces adjacent to dwellings (mobile or fixed) and sometimes

Tourist market, Place du Palais Royal, Paris. Temporary and seasonal events like this transform the character and use of urban spaces on a daily basis even though the infrastructure at the city level is relatively fixed.

in neutral locations determined by geography or proximity to settlements or group boundaries. Meetings, then and now, might take place for commerce (markets and trading); for entertainment (fairs, performance and sports); for the settlement of disputes (trials, debates and battles).[2]

Historic meeting places have been adopted as locations of great significance and are often the most important spaces in a city – squares and piazzas are used for great public events as well as the casual, but no less important, everyday activities. A range of mobile and temporary building types have been created over the centuries to support such events, and many are still used today, for example market stalls, performance stages and seating, canteens and eating-places. A town square can be used as a car park during the week, a food market on Saturday, for a public concert on Sunday and to announce a new mayor after an election. It is an adaptable space defined sufficiently by its boundaries, but unrestricted enough to allow access. It is serviced with lighting, power and drainage to accommodate a range of ancillary equipment that can change its character sufficiently to enable it to fulfil its changing role. Of equal importance is its ability to be adaptable enough to allow these different roles to become attached to its image (or even replace it) in the memory of the user. However, its identity as a specific place where the

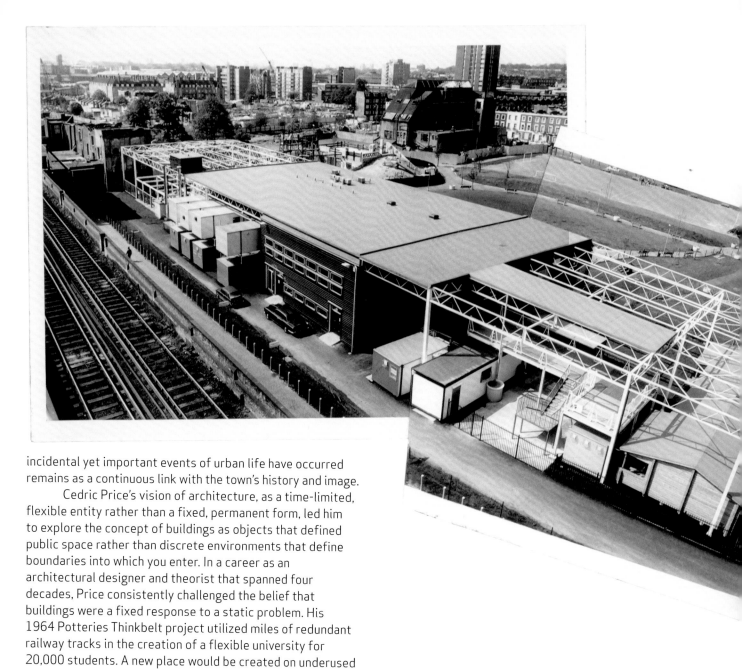

incidental yet important events of urban life have occurred remains as a continuous link with the town's history and image.

Cedric Price's vision of architecture, as a time-limited, flexible entity rather than a fixed, permanent form, led him to explore the concept of buildings as objects that defined public space rather than discrete environments that define boundaries into which you enter. In a career as an architectural designer and theorist that spanned four decades, Price consistently challenged the belief that buildings were a fixed response to a static problem. His 1964 Potteries Thinkbelt project utilized miles of redundant railway tracks in the creation of a flexible university for 20,000 students. A new place would be created on underused industrial land with prefabricated and mobile facilities, redefining not only the way this specific location was viewed, but also the idea of what a university might be.

From 1971 Price was able to build his most resolved vision of what responsive architecture might be – Kentish Town Inter-Action Centre in London. Based on his earlier idea for The Fun Palace (1960–1), it included an unenclosed steel frame in which travelling cranes could be used to locate prefabricated walls, stairs and service modules as determined by the user. The Kentish Town building consisted of a 'fundamental stage' into which the individuals of the Inter-Action Trust could locate a range of community

**Inter-Action Centre, Kentish Town,
London, UK, 1971–9: Cedric Price.**

facilities. These included workshops, studies, offices, a club and a pre-school playgroup. The open steel frame formed an infrastructure around which prefabricated elements could be placed and also identified a new external street and urban square. Critical to Price's thinking was that the structure would have a limited life of 20 years, although within that period it would be in a state of continuous change. Price's ideas were important influences on a younger generation of architects, notably Peter Cook of Archigram and Richard Rogers.

Price's Inter-Action Centre was an amalgam of external and internal space, much of it intended to be open to public use. Meeting places within building environments are more specific than public spaces, however, and are still designed for use by different sorts of people with different agendas and different tasks to perform. Communication, discussion, decision-making, performance and ceremonies take place in spaces designed to hold from ten to 10,000 people and beyond. Here, the specific agenda of the host building can determine the form of the space, though even this is now being challenged. Some meeting spaces are specifically designed to avoid flexibility so that a determined pattern of use can be established. Typical of this type are religious buildings, government buildings and courts. This is so that the continuity of the institution and/or the ritual can take precedence over the debate. In this way, architecture is used

**The Fun Palace, unrealized project
for East London, UK, 1960–1:
Cedric Price.**

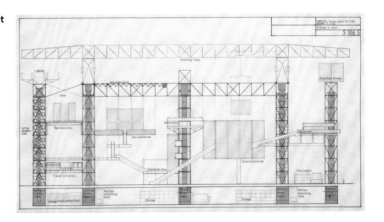

to help determine the character and limits of the events the building hosts. However, some types of meeting spaces, which previously could be placed in this category, are now challenging their traditional architectural pattern and moving towards a much more flexible system.

Workplaces are the most important buildings that people occupy outside the home. The design of office buildings has changed significantly in the search for more creative ways of organizing work, recognizing a range of social and psychological factors that improve the experience for workers and quality of output for employers. Offices are frequently designed as non-specific, speculative development. The perception is that this activity can be supported purely by providing space and IT connections. However, offices can also benefit from more dedicated responses to the need for change.

One of the most famous innovative office buildings was the result of a brief from a new company that set out to create a different sort of environment for their developing business.[3] In 1967, the influential architect and theorist Herman Hertzberger began the design of new offices for the insurance company Centraal Beheer in Appeldoorn, the Netherlands. He adhered to the philosophy of 'spatial possibility' in which buildings provided frameworks that the users could adapt to their own requirements. Hertzberger

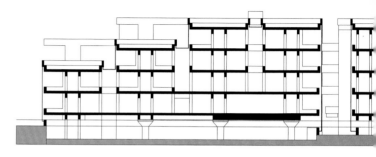

Section

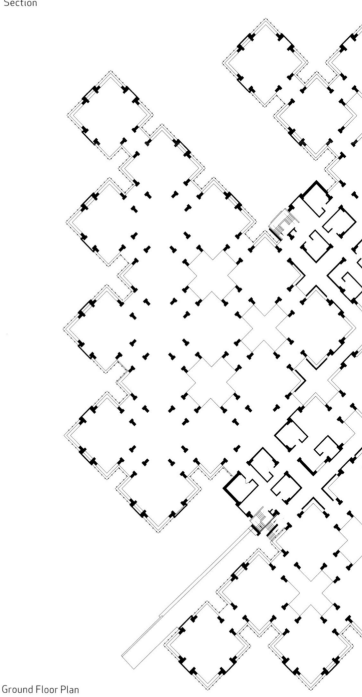

Ground Floor Plan

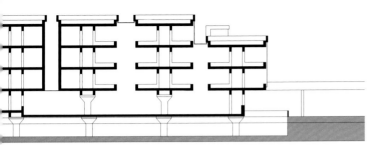

Centraal Beheer, Appeldoorn, the Netherlands, 1967–72: Herman Hertzberger.

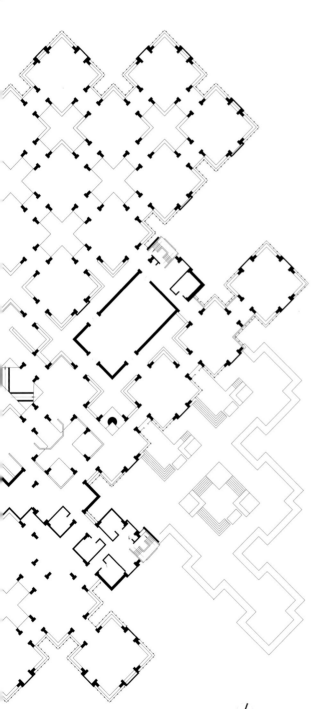

/

employed this concept on a range of building types including housing but this office was his best-known success. The building consists of a precast concrete, modular structure organized around a system of equal-sized spaces that could be linked together in many different ways to allow varying patterns of use.[4] It has been described as 'an organizational instrument', the purpose of which was to assist the company by providing staff with a creative environment that increased the opportunity for informal contact and openness to varied ways of use. Indeed, the rough concrete masonry of the building gave it a physical workmanlike image, which contradicts the slick corporate presence that many administrative buildings project. This lack of hierarchy extended to the exterior, which lacks the formalizing order that is usual in office buildings. Nevertheless, staff adopted the building, decorating it with their own possessions and giving the interior the ambience of a lived-in community rather than an office building. In 1994, the now successful and growing company commissioned a substantial extension to house 1,200 staff. Hertzberger's original ideas about the importance of 'meeting' areas were reinforced by the inclusion of 48 separate spaces, both formal and informal, for this purpose.

Frank Gehry's Stata Center (2005) in Cambridge, Massachusetts, was a replacement for MIT's Building 90

built during World War II. The facility was nicknamed 'The Magic Incubator' owing to the many inventions that have emerged from those who work inside. The new building has been designed specifically to respond to the freethinking agenda necessary for breakthroughs in the field of computers, information and intelligence studies. After lengthy discussions with its future users Gehry designed a building that featured suites of rooms that were purposely not clearly defined or rigidly separated. He also built in the possibility for reconfiguration of the spaces to create a stimulating and flexible environment. The design began with a three-dimensional physical model, created in relation to its surrounding buildings, which was then gradually changed in response to interior rearrangements. The building interior is stimulating and informal – corridors expand into lounge areas and meeting spaces, and views through to other offices, laboratories and the exterior occur at every turn. The ground floor is a multi-height street with meeting spaces, lecture rooms, a café, wall-high notice boards and IT spaces integrated into the circulation. Unlike Hertzberger's office, Gehry's building rejects the understandable organizational layout that is intended to encourage easy adoption by its users. Instead Gehry stimulates reaction and response by asserting an especially challenging architectural environment on the user. It is restless, hyperactive,

Stata Center, Cambridge, Mass., USA, 2005: Frank Gehry.

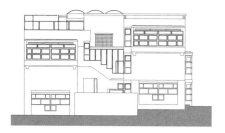

West Elevation

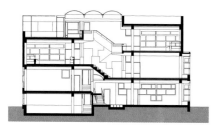

Section

reactive design that is intended to provoke response rather than simply allowing it to happen.

Another familiar area where change is occurring is in schools. The classroom was once an extremely hierarchical space, teacher to the front and established on a podium, children at a lower level sitting behind rows of desks. Modern classroom design, however, favours group working with zoned spaces for different activities and a roaming teacher. This has in turn affected the linking spaces (once corridors) which have now become available for use in a much more flexible manner depending on the time of day or date in the academic year. Hertzberger's 1980 Willemspark School building in Amsterdam was a forecast of a much more interactive teaching environment in which the building's spaces and its detailed form could stimulate responses from pupils and staff both during class and play. A simple, formal plan of nine interlocking squares is carefully articulated by varying the levels between the two sides of the building. Rich but robust details provide myriad opportunities for interpretive use; for example, the central hallway can alternatively be an assembly area, a theatre, a playroom or a place for individual study.

Cartwright Pickard's 2004 project for a Freeform Modular School has been planned to provide flexibility in its spaces, but it also incorporates a modular construction system, designed in collaboration with modular building

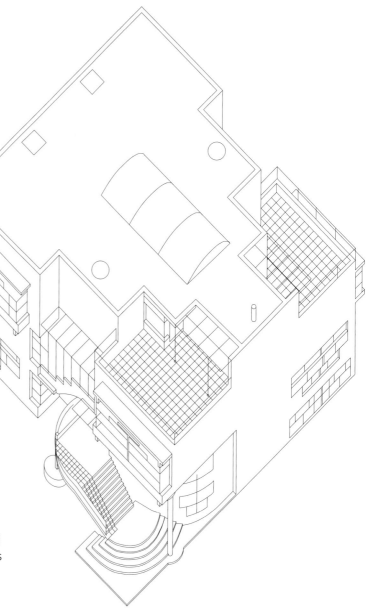

Willemspark School, Amsterdam, the Netherlands, 1980: Herman Hertzberger.

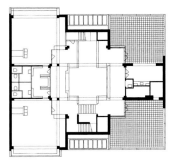

Third Floor Plan

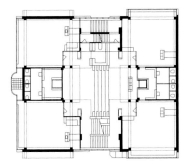

Second Floor Plan

First Floor Plan

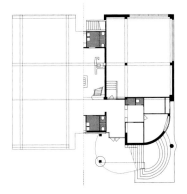

Ground Floor Plan

Freeform Modular School project, UK, 2004: Cartwright Pickard and Yorkon.

manufacturer Yorkon, to take advantage of prefabricated manufacturing techniques. The design utilizes modules that are pre-manufactured for speed of site erection. These can be arranged in different ways to provide various sized classroom areas or can be grouped in clusters to create a variety of zones within the school, each having an atrium space for shared learning and interaction. The clusters can also be secured for out-of hours use, thus providing greater flexibility in the use of the entire building.

One building that has been designed solely around the concept of 'meeting place' is FTL Design Engineering Studio's AT&T Global Olympic Village, created for the 1996 Olympic Games in Atlanta, USA. Though most of the facilities built for Olympic games are designed to be part of an urban improvement programme that will subsequently form new, improved facilities for local people, there are some functions that cannot be easily reassigned to new use. In this case temporary buildings are required; or if the function can be duplicated at similar future events, portable architecture may result. The AT&T Global Olympic Village's primary function was to be a public international communications facility that would provide a service for both the athletes and the visitors to phone, fax and e-mail home. Linked to this global 'meeting' was the function of local public relations and social events so that the building also contained informal seating areas, a restaurant and conference suites.

The architecture was designed as a communication tool in itself. It consisted of a pair of membrane-clad pavilions, formed from steel portal frames surmounting a rigid two-storey-high base. The membrane was used as a screen, with special computer-controlled projectors designed to correct images so that they could display events from the show or elsewhere in the stadium onto the curved surface without distortion. The building formed the backdrop to the main performance stage where each evening shows took place to entertain the 100,000-plus Olympic crowd and millions around the world through a live TV feed. The agenda of the AT&T Village therefore spanned between a local one, as a meeting place and communications focus point, and a wider one, as a cultural icon to be seen as part of the setting for an event of worldwide interest.

Cultural buildings are key in establishing identity for a community, be it at local, city or national level. The role of the contemporary cultural building is, however, undergoing change. Museums, once seen as repositories for precious objects, are now perceived as places of entertainment and interaction as well as education and research. Theatres and concert halls also have a remit to be accessible to a much wider range of interests. These institutions have a role in

AT&T Global Olympic Village, Atlanta, USA, 1996: FTL Design Engineering Studio.

generating income through tourism, and consequently have a responsibility for an impact that extends beyond their cultural role into urban regeneration. This has led to substantial changes in the way these buildings are used with a much greater range of activities taking place within them.

The Pompidou Centre (also known as the Beaubourg Cultural Centre) in Paris was designed by Renzo Piano and Richard Rogers and built in 1977 with the specific ambition of being a multi-media arts complex. The original brief was to provide a 'Cultural Centre for Paris', which was interpreted by the architects to be a 'Live Centre of Information and Entertainment'. Nevertheless, the competition brief was to design a building that contained a museum of modern art, a reference library, a centre for industrial design and a centre for music and acoustic research. Piano and Rogers expanded this from something aimed at the art specialist to include the casual visitor, the local resident and the tourist, by creating a 'truly dynamic meeting place where activities would overlap in flexible, well-serviced spaces, a people's centre, a university of the street reflecting the constantly changing needs of users.'[5] The result is a celebrated icon of High-Tech architecture – complex, colourful, energetic and quite unique.

The design was intended to be expressive of change as well as its realization in practical terms. Key to its concept was the flexible layout of the building, with services and

Pompidou Centre, Paris, France,
1977: Piano and Rogers.

access distributed around the perimeter to allow completely open floor plates that could be rearranged in any manner. The expressive, bolt-together structure was layered with clipped-on and colour-coded access and service elements – people were meant to understand from its appearance the process of architecture as an enabler for freedom of activity and use. External moving escalators and lifts gave activity and mobility to the façade. Internally, a hierarchy of flexibility was built into the facility – small, light-weight partitions that could be moved in a minute, and the larger museum partitions that could be moved within an hour. The firewalls were more difficult to relocate, but they were still bolted in place to provide the potential for significant change. Services were provided at floor and ceiling level over the vast 169 x 48 metre (555 x 158 foot) floors.

As well as its iconic architectural impact, the effect of the building on the surrounding area was also significant. It completely changed the nature of its neighbourhood through the physical introduction of a new open space and new routes to the locality, and also through the economic and cultural changes it brought. This one, hugely successful building was the catalyst that changed a neglected and undesirable neighbourhood into a vibrant and developing community. The fact that it was also a revolutionary building in constructional, aesthetic and operational terms had a

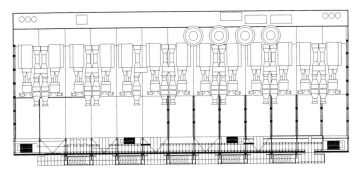

Roof Plan

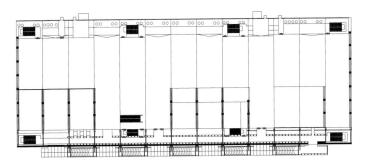

Top Floor Plan

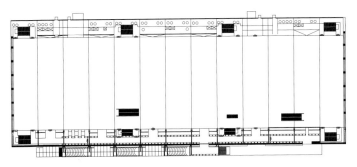

Second Floor Plan

Cross Section

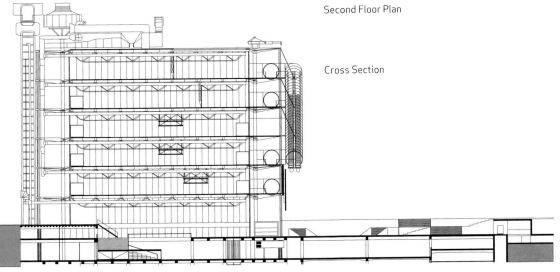

significant bearing on its impact, which extends into the city of Paris and beyond.[6]

Toyo Ito's Sendai Mediatheque (2000) has had a similar extended impact that, although less dramatic, is perhaps no less significant in that it is a more sensitive approach, tuned to local, rather than international, audiences. Though designed for a specific site with a dedicated limited function, this building has had an important effect on both its neighbourhood within the city of Sendai and the city's image as communicated to the rest of Japan. The site for the Mediatheque is on an extension of one of the city's main roads, but some distance away from the main commercial and business district. The building's presence and its success in attracting local and visiting users has extended the commercial viability of the street so that many new businesses have now opened there.

The building consists of a series of flat floor plates, surrounded by an opaque and clear glass wall and supported by a group of lattice 'trees' made from steel tubes of different, undulating shapes. The centre of each 'tree' has been left open to allow light and space to move between the levels of the building, though some of them also contain lifts and services. Each floor has different, though linked, uses – library, information technology centre, exhibition spaces, meeting rooms, café and shop. All the spaces are fully

Sendai Mediatheque, Japan, 2000: Toyo Ito.

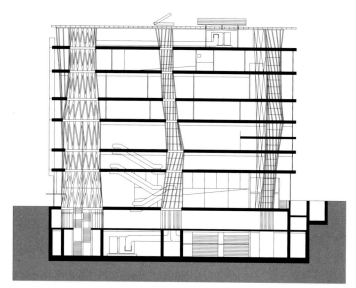

Section

**Sendai Mediatheque, Japan, 2000:
Toyo Ito.**

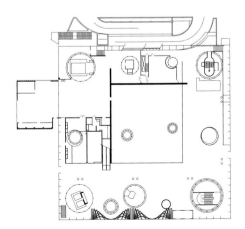

Ground Floor Plan

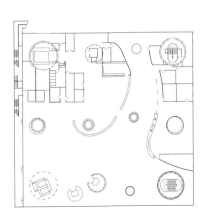

First Floor Plan

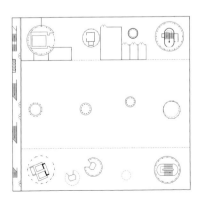

Fifth Floor Plan

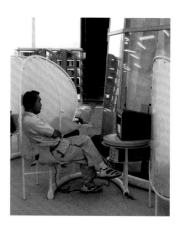

Sendai Mediatheque, Japan, 2000: Toyo Ito.

accessible within the building and are open plan wherever possible – a large number are multi-functional. Many of the furnishings and partitions are easily movable. It is easy to shape a personally tuned visit: to browse books and magazines; eavesdrop on people watching films in open-plan booths; take a flower-arranging class; or visit an art exhibition. Yet all the time you are also constantly aware of the city around you, the various levels of the building providing different views as you ascend to the top floor where the roofscape opens up to the countryside beyond. Ito has stated that the Mediatheque was the first building in which he successfully fused his ideas about creating beautiful spaces that are also flexible enough for adaptation and change, based on experience and developing demands.

Buildings designed for cultural purposes often have significant impact in that they are generally required to be exemplary designs with commissions carried out by important designers to ambitious briefs. Exhibition and special event structures also draw more attention than purely functional, non-public buildings for the same reason – indeed the requirement to have a publicity-generating agenda can be a significant part of the brief.

One example where experimental building can have a significant impact is the Expo, a regular international showcase of commerce and industry that is held in a different

country each time. The purpose of an Expo is to provide a
venue for countries to communicate their willingness and
ability to take part in the global business community. Planned
years in advance, they are usually based close to a major city.
The host usually takes the opportunity to undertake a major
infrastructure programme that will initially provide the
framework for the event but will also lead to regeneration
of the area in future years. Public transport and road links,
services, support buildings and planning for post-Expo use
are all involved. Government organizations (such as the UK
Department of Trade and Industry) negotiate the site for
their temporary pavilion, which is erected shortly before the
six-month-long event begins. A difficult balance must then be
established between expenditure on what is almost certainly
going to be a temporary facility and the ambition to make a
quality product. The Expo is the present-day relation of the
Great Exhibitions in London (1851) and Paris (1899), which
left important legacies for these cities in the form of the
Crystal Palace in London (destroyed by fire in 1936) and the
Eiffel Tower in Paris. Contemporary Expos do not usually
result in such a high level of investment as the majority of the
buildings are impermanent and there is a powerful argument
that temporary structures are not only economically unviable,
but also ecologically questionable. For this reason, recent
Expos have frequently included buildings that have strived

British Pavilion, Expo 92, Seville, Spain, 1991: Nicholas Grimshaw.

for maximum effect using innovative, reusable strategies that allow a change in purpose after the Expo is over.

The British Pavilion at Expo 92 in Seville, Spain, was designed to be a completely reusable structure. Designed by Nicholas Grimshaw with engineers Arup, it was the result of a limited competition created in partnership with British Steel. The building was manufactured in the UK and shipped to the site in Spain. It was designed with a logical erection process utilizing a series of frames that braced each other as they were assembled. Solar panels powered a cooling 'water wall' that was necessary in the extreme heat of the Andalusian summer. Each of the solar-power/pump assemblies was designed to be reused after the event to provide power for villages in the developing world.[7] With water-lined walls on one side and translucent fabric on the other, the architecture communicated a potent image of a great engineering nation, embedded in a trading maritime history. The building undoubtedly possessed an impressive high-quality, high-technology image that was strongly reminiscent of its ancestor, Paxton's Crystal Palace. However, it is still questionable whether such a heavy-weight solution to a temporary and mobile problem is appropriate due to the high cost of transportation and re-erection.

Shigeru Ban took a more sustainable approach in his design for the Japan Pavilion at Expo 2000 in Hanover,

Germany. Ban created a recyclable structure made primarily of paper tubes and a thin timber lattice. It was also clad with a paper-based roof membrane, although an additional plastic layer was added in response to German Building Authority requirements. The main space was left open to reveal the delicate latticework of the structure against the translucent paper skin. Loose-laid stone aggregates and reusable containers were also incorporated in the completely recyclable facility. As with the Expo 92 British Pavilion, the building itself became the principal exhibit of its nation's engineering and industrial prowess.

From these examples it can be seen that the problem of providing flexibility in building design is a complex balancing of advantages. In some cases the decision to take a flexible approach has a critical impact on the character of the project and the way in which problems can be solved. Perhaps the most ambitious buildings that are specifically designed to be flexible are those that accommodate many thousands of people for public events. Stadium design in particular has become more sophisticated as the revenues generated from sports have become greater. This has resulted in a demand for much larger venues, but in order to fund them it has become a common feature for them to become multi-purpose, staging other events as well as those associated with their core purpose. Understandably, this can also lead to conflict.

Japan Pavilion, Expo 2000, Hanover, Germany, 1999: Shigeru Ban.

Sports activities are traditionally carried out in the open air on turf fields – seasonal conditions are an important component in the outcome of the game. In addition, grass is a living surface that requires light, air and moisture to survive. The traditional external stadium provided shelter for the spectators, but left the playing surface exposed to the elements. However, sports stadia are now more frequently required to host music concerts or large conventions, both of which are not compatible with grass surfaces and operate far better in a sheltered space.

Two primary solutions have been developed to allow stadia to cope with these flexibility issues – the opening roof and the rollout field. Opening roof stadia are impressive feats of engineering, requiring large-span, mechanically operated structures that are mobile. The first substantial opening roof design was the Toronto SkyDome (now Rogers Centre) built in 1989, designed by architect Rod Robbie and structural engineer Mike Allan. The SkyDome is the home of the Canadian baseball team the Blue Jays, but it is also a multi-functional leisure venue hosting a wide range of other events including American football and soccer games. The stadium has a range of facilities within the same building, including restaurants, a television studio, health centre, concert hall, conference centre, and a 350-bed hotel (70 of the rooms actually look onto the pitch). Because of the many purposes the building

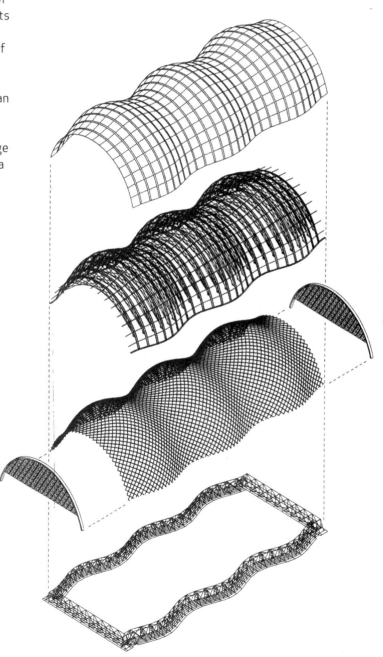

Japan Pavilion, Expo 2000, Hanover, Germany, 1999: Shigeru Ban.
Exploded axonometric showing the three structural layers of the roof: paper tubes, timber and paper skin.

TSA/Cardinals Stadium, Glendale, Arizona, USA, 1997–2006: Eisenman Architects.

is used for, its fast conversion time and its tight urban site, it was unfeasible to use natural grass for the pitch. The conversion of the playing field into a multi-function bare floor takes eight hours and from a baseball to football layout it takes 16 hours. Of the 57,000 seats, over half can change position depending on the activity that is taking place. The key to the building's multi-functional capability, however, is the opening roof. This consists of three moving segments – tubular steel arches that span up to 205 metres (673 foot) in width and 87 metres (284 foot) high and that slide and rotate into a stack at the north end of the stadium in 20 minutes. When fully retracted, 90 per cent of the seats are open to the sky, as is most of the 3.2 hectares (7.9 acres) of space. In 1997, a record year, it was in use for 302 days and seated a total of 4.5 million people.

Since the SkyDome many stadia have been built with opening roofs, but with more site area available North America's newest venue of this type will have both an opening roof and a rollout field. Peter Eisenman's design for the Arizona Cardinals' stadium in Glendale, Arizona was begun in June 2003 and completed in 2006. The building is designed to host the most prestigious American football events, including the SuperBowl, but it is also a major conference and special event venue. Eisenman's exterior design, a vertically slotted façade, takes its precedent from the form of the local Barrel

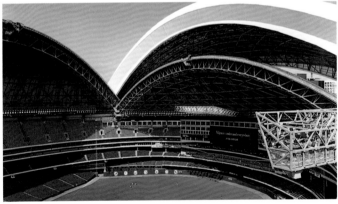

SkyDome Stadium, Toronto, Canada, 1989: RAN Consortium Architects and Engineers. A Partnership of Corporations: Robbie / Young + Wright Architects Inc. Adjeleian Allen Rubeli Limited, Consulting Engineers. NORR Limited, Architects & Engineers.

Matsumoto Performing Arts Centre,
Matsumoto, Japan, 2004: Toyo Ito.

Flexible Community

Cactus, but the focus of interest is the engineering. The roof is built in two fabric-covered panels that retract to uncover the entire playing field. The stadium's natural grass field rolls outside the stadium, where it will stay most of the year for growth and maintenance. The permanent concrete floor inside has an embedded service grid to allow maximum flexibility for trade shows and concerts. This 63,000 permanent-seat stadium (all air-conditioned) can be expanded to 73,000 for special events. A 14,000-space car park is close by, with a further 12,000 spaces within one mile (1.6 kilometres).

Many different strategies are used in many different building types, so is it possible to establish what are the most important elements in enabling flexibility? Though such diverse solutions are not easily categorized, a number of key, common factors can be identified. In order to do this it is useful to examine in detail one building that has been designed with these factors embedded into its conceptual approach and its detailed execution.

Toyo Ito's design for the Matsumoto Performing Arts Centre in Matsumoto, Nagano Prefecture, Japan (opened in 2004) was chosen in competition against ten other teams by a unanimous panel that included a client who had already thought very hard about the building's function and siting. The Centre's main programme is focused around two theatres, with 240 and 1,800 seats respectively, and a range of rehearsal spaces, studios, workshops and a restaurant. The large hall is a key venue for the annual opera performances staged during the Saito Kinen Festival that is held each summer, though it also accommodates a wide range of other performances. The small hall is principally a community theatre and is used by the people of Matsumoto rather than professionals. The site is a difficult one. It is long and thin, surrounded by nondescript buildings and car parks, and its presence on the main street is restricted to its smallest end. Furthermore, the high ground-water in the area (many local buildings still use individual wells for water supply) meant that below-ground building was not possible. The Centre's location has similarities with the Sendai Mediatheque, the street being an extension of one that runs to the city centre. However, it is currently without any buildings of significant merit or public functions.

Ito's response to this range of problems had to deal with two critical issues. The first, not untypical of many large, new urban buildings, is how to deal with situating such a building effectively alongside its neighbours while creating a civic presence for an important public function. Normally theatres have a hierarchical presence on the site: front of house with the entrance, circulation and hospitality facilities at the street access side; back of house with the deliveries, workshops and rehearsal rooms at the rear. This particular site made this difficult to achieve so the designers situated the main theatre in the centre of the site and the auditorium to the rear, with the entrance, minor theatre and rehearsal rooms to the front. This unusual disposition also helped to solve Ito's other main objective – to create a building that would be adopted by its users and visitors and be capable of adaptation and response to their developing needs.

Entry into the Matsumoto Performing Arts Centre is into a large, multi-level space with the box office and reception to one side and a curved wall on the opposite one that flows beside a gently ramped stairway and travelator leading to the upper floor. The visitor ascends through this space in a sweeping movement that gradually opens out into a linear volume – Ito has dubbed this the 'theatre park'. In front is the rear wall of the main auditorium; this is a large, glass partition that gives a view down to the stage. Behind, the square box of the small theatre protrudes into the space and beyond this is the restaurant that faces onto the street. The curved wall encircles all the public spaces of the building in an organic form. It is a continuous volume that provides access to both theatre auditoria, restaurant, foyer and entrance and has an ambiguous and amorphous character. Nevertheless, it also possesses a distinct sense of place in its own right. On top of this space is a public roof garden towards which the rehearsal rooms face.

Though the large spaces of this building are very simple in form, great care has gone into their detailed design.

The carpeted floor has been graphically processed to indicate changes in shade in relation to furniture and building structure. The colour patterns in the auditoria form a shaded matrix that visually reflects the acoustic and artificial illumination qualities of the space. Most remarkable is the great curved wall, which is made from smooth-finished glass-reinforced concrete panels with seven kinds of recycled glass inlaid in a random pattern of lozenge shapes. This provides a soft, natural, diffused light and also a unique wall surface that is smooth and continuous. Its curving contour harmonizes with the pattern and articulated colour shading of the other interior surfaces.

This building exhibits Ito's approach to allowing the users to respond and adapt the functionality of the architecture in a number of new and sophisticated ways. He creates forms and spaces that utilize new technology to expand the possibilities of what the building can do and also to increase its capacity to adapt to future changes. He communicates ideas about the architecture in a clear and direct manner to its occupants so that the messages can be understood by them and developed further. In creating a building that responds to very specific problems in a unique way, he creates a form of architecture that is special to its site and programme. There are four special ways in which this particular design has responded to the issue of creating flexible architecture that have general application:

Matsumoto Performing Arts Centre,
Matsumoto, Japan, 2004: Toyo Ito.

Transformable Elements: Spaces that are nominally
dedicated to a specific function, thereby fulfilling the present
brief for the building, are also designed to support and even
encourage other methods of use. The large theatre has a
ceiling that can be lowered to give different acoustic
conditions or a more intimate auditorium. Behind the
stage there is a large area of adaptable seating to allow for
different audience perspectives or the incorporation of an
on-stage choir. The backstage area has a glass wall to allow
views into the auditorium from behind a performance. The
small theatre has an extendable stage, removable seating and
a choice of natural lighting or full blackout for different types
of performance. These transformable elements encourage
the users of the building to be creative in finding ways to
help it serve their needs.

Adaptable Spaces: The building makes use of space
in a multi-functional way. All theatres need breakout space
from the auditorium to allow the audience to circulate from
entrance to bar to performance. The Centre's two theatres
merge this space into a continuous, fluid volume that
expresses no particular function, but instead suggests many
– extra informal performance space, an exhibition space and
an area for meetings and events. The servicing of this
environment, in terms of natural and artificial light, allows for
different sorts of activities to take place. The theatre park is

**Matsumoto Performing Arts Centre,
Matsumoto, Japan, 2004: Toyo Ito.**

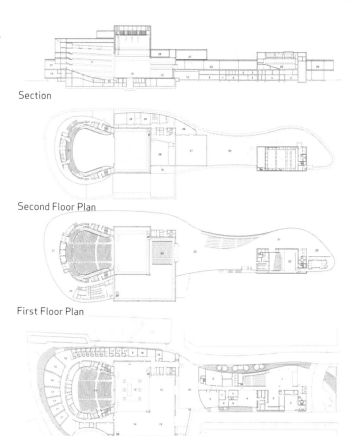

Section

Second Floor Plan

First Floor Plan

Ground Floor Plan

a space where many diverse events can happen – an art show, a conference, a crafts workshop, a dance or even a wedding.

Interactive Operation: The careful planning and organization of spaces within the building design encourages greater freedom of movement for the visitor and increased interaction with the user. As a community building it is essential that local people feel they have access to the facility. Like the Sendai Mediatheque, Ito has created a series of interconnected spaces, but it is a more difficult task considering the enclosed functions of some of the spaces required in the Matsumoto programme. This has been done by creating new sorts of spaces that are genuinely valuable public areas from what would normally be identified solely as a circulation area. The theatre park is the most important of these, connecting readily accessible functions, such as the entrance, box office and restaurant, with the theatres. However, the roof garden is also important in this regard, providing views into the rehearsal rooms and back over the city and its surroundings. The glass walls to the rear of the theatre and the studio provide unique opportunities for the visitor to interact with the artist outside of the formal performance event. The public are also visible from the street, primarily in the restaurant and the roof garden, communicating to the passer-by that this is a readily accessible building. The building design actively encourages people to come in and see what is happening and then to use it in many different ways.

Movable Elements: The building's theatre park provides a surface on which different mobile components, including ticket desks, wardrobes, catering and concession stands, chairs and tables, stages and presentation equipment, can be located to organize the space. Entry routes can be realigned; areas of privacy identified; and exhibitions, informal performances and special events accommodated.

Ito's Matsumoto Performing Arts Centre is a building that establishes cultural identity for the people of the city it serves, and thereby permanence and continuity, and has allowed, and even promoted, the opportunity for changing uses from the day it opened. It is designed to respect the wishes and needs of the people for whom it has been built – both the professionals who will operate and utilize the building and the community who will also make use of its facilities as audiences or performers. Its potential for success lies in the fact that it has been designed to be a responsive tool, one that also has its own distinctive character. The measure of the building's achievement, and of the methods it uses to deliver its flexible agenda, will be in the way its use develops over years to come.

1 John Habraken, *Supports: An Alternative to Mass Housing* (1961), new edition, Seattle, 1999.
2 In addition, gatherings may have happened for religious reasons, but because of their associated rituals they (like a few other specific events) have now adopted a more rigid structure that is the antithesis of the freedom that is at the heart of the flexible use of space.
3 'The basic requirements of an office building may well be simple enough in principle, but it was this need for adaptability that led to the complexity of the commission. Constant changes occur within the organization, thereby requiring frequent adjustments to the size of the different departments. The building must be capable of accommodating these internal forces, while the building as a whole must continue to function in every respect and at all times.' Arnulf Lüchinger (ed.), *Herman Hertzberger: Buildings and Projects*, The Hague, 1987, p.87.
4 See Hugh Anderson, 'Centraal Beheer Revisited' in *Architectural Review*, vol.196, no.1174, December 1994, pp.72–8.
5 Barbara Cole and Ruth Rogers (eds.), *Richard Rogers Architects*, Architectural Monographs, London, 1985, p.91.
6 See Robert Kronenburg, *Spirit of the Machine*, Chichester, 2001, p.39. Though the potent image of the architecture remains, a recent extensive refurbishment has compromised some of the ideals of the original concept, largely due to security concerns.
7 The building was dismantled and shipped home to the UK after the Expo, where a developer purchased but never reused it in its recognizable form.

Flexible Architecture

Is there a need to radically review the characteristics of contemporary architecture? The architects of a hundred years ago reacted to the pressures of an emerging global culture, in part at least, through the adoption of international influences in the way they designed buildings. Even today, the way in which buildings are delivered is primarily dependent on local and regional factors. This is, in itself, not a problem; in fact it is extremely appropriate because local situations must be taken into account to establish relevant and identifiable architecture. However, global issues are also now more important than they have ever been – international economic, political and ecological factors shape the way the world operates. Transcontinental trade, mass instant communication and global media impact on everyone's life, from the smallest item that we buy in the supermarket to how we perceive our place as individuals in our community, our nation, our world.

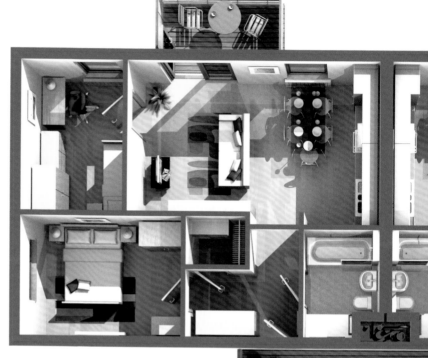

BoKlok Housing, Sweden, 2000:
IKEA and Ahiström Arkitektbyrä.

Though building delivery is still local, the ideas and the markets that shape that delivery are international. Early twentieth-century modernists who subscribed to the International Style and Le Corbusier's description of the house as a 'machine for living' ostensibly sought to find a new efficiency in buildings that would deliver health and happiness through a mixture of fresh air, indoor plumbing and a modern aesthetic. They believed that this was a revolution that would affect the way all buildings were built, and in many ways it has, although not with the universal stylistic impact they envisaged.

Contemporary architecture contains many machines both as discrete objects and as part of a building's services. This characteristic is likely to intensify in the future rather than decline. However, though new buildings may utilize more sophisticated and more numerous technological features in the future, the way a building is used is fundamentally unlike a machine's use. Although we manipulate the elements and controls of a building, it cannot be considered in the same way as, for example, a CD player or a washing machine. A house is cared for; we clean it, maintain it and decorate it, and in return it provides for our psychological as well as our physical needs. In 1960, the architectural historian Reyner Banham wrote an article for the *Architectural Review* in which he stated: 'The functionalist slogan, "the house is a

machine for living" is not productive because it begins by presupposing the idea of the house'.[1] Banham's question was synonymous with what many of the experimental architects, who were to influence the course of architecture over the next two decades and beyond, tried to address – but is it still relevant today? Well … yes and no! Yes, because as Heidegger recognized a sense of place is not established by just building, but by any method human beings can use to recognize what place is. No, because a building is not something that just makes us physically comfortable, it also has a cultural, aesthetic and psychological role, and the making of a physical place (sometimes that may even be a little uncomfortable) is still a good way to establish place.

The possibilities available for architectural design have been increased by the advance of technology. However, it has not always been clear in what way that advance could be best used to make better buildings. As the architect and theorist Adolf Loos stated: 'There is no point in inventing anything unless it is an improvement'.[2] Often advances are first seen in another field and then adapted by designers into architecture. Advances in architectural technology do make more building forms available to the designer, but there are other factors that affect the generation of those forms and they are usually more powerful, such as economic, social, cultural and aesthetic issues. Technology is a driving force, but it tends to drive society first and architecture, as its servant, follows behind.

The need for adaptable architecture supports the servant role, as it has done for most of human history. A flexible approach to our environment is now necessary for a wide range of reasons: 24-hour work patterns based in the home; changing family size and groupings; ecological issues that are questioning the desirability of commuting; lifestyle issues that envisage a more fulfilling personal life; and the possibility of remote working due to communications technology. So, what are the characteristics of an architecture that is fully adaptable to this fluctuating living and working pattern? Easily recognizable now is the interdependence of architecture, furniture, appliances, clothing, vehicles and consumables – all the acquired aspects of modern life. At one level this is simply fashion and marketing – indeed architecture is continually used to sell associated products as part of a lifestyle. But it is also about creating an identifiable picture of yourself as an individual, and if that is by the purchase of expensive, fashionable designer wear, and you can afford it, then that is 'you'. However, it can also be about things of personal significance, acquired over a lifetime, that have little commercial value – for example Charles and Ray Eames' very individual collection of craft and art objects that cost very little to buy. Their

**BoKlok Housing, Sweden, 2000:
IKEA and Ahiström Arkitektbyrä.**

1948 house was inspired by this same sensibility and, because it was extensively published at an international level and celebrated in films and books by the Eames themselves, has become a stylistic icon.

The 'modern style' object purveyors like IKEA (Sweden), MUJI (Japan) and Habitat (UK) are the contemporary sponsors of the new fashion-conscious home, containing mass-produced, self-tuned, modular products with potentially limitless variations. IKEA (who also own Habitat) are the largest furniture retailer in the world and their BoKlok (meaning 'smart living' in Swedish) housing is aimed at broadly the same group of people who buy their home furnishings. BoKlok has gone beyond the prototype stage and several thousand homes have been provided in Sweden with plans to supply markets in Norway, Poland and the UK. Though economy restricts the variety of current building projects, these are designer objects that offer a new choice to house buyers. But are their building proposals only publicity attractors like the Dymaxion House and the rest of the 'houses of the future'?

The idea focuses on economy rather than innovation in construction and the novelty is to be found in the way it is marketed and delivered. The homes are built in small groups of four or five buildings using a standardized prefabricated timber frame that can be erected in four days, though in-situ

Variomatic House, the Netherlands,
2000: Kas Oosterhuis.

work means the total build is closer to four months. Standard,
Scandinavian windows and doors are used, and details and
finishes are to regulation standards. As this is clearly budget
housing, the architectural style and interior layout is pretty
unremarkable, though purchase does include an IKEA
furniture voucher and a two-hour session with an interior
design consultant! Perhaps more useful is a partnership with
a sympathetic financial organization (a Housing Association
in the UK) to provide low-interest loans. What is on offer,
therefore, is affordable, contemporary design: a real
alternative for many buyers especially as IKEA's product is
aimed specifically at people with low to medium household
incomes. It must be acknowledged, however, that there must
be at least some risk to the consumers' individual freedom in
relinquishing total control of their entire environment to a
single, large, commercial enterprise.[3]

The risk of non-domestic architecture falling under
the spell of style-consciousness, rather than quality and
appropriateness, is just as strong. Though there is no doubt
that the most famous contemporary designers have reached
their position as design icons because of the quality of their
work, there is also a sense that their very success has led to
questionable reasons for commissioning them. At one point it
seemed that every city in the world would eventually possess
a museum designed by Richard Meier ... until Frank Gehry

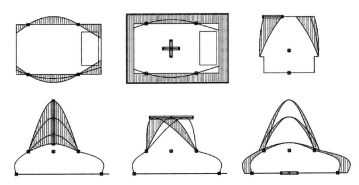

Variomatic House, the Netherlands, 2000: Kas Oosterhuis.
Design drawings showing options for form, plan and cladding.

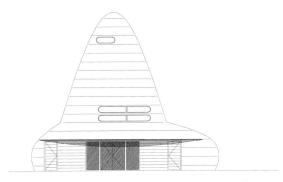

Elevation

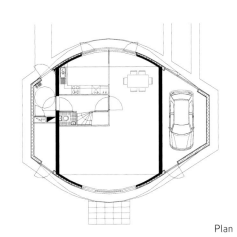

Plan

started to get the commissions. It is not that these architects are necessarily producing bad buildings, but just the sense that until a city has its 'Meier' or its 'Gehry' it is not on the cultural map. Is this just recognition at last that architecture really matters when regenerating our cities, or is it another aspect of the creeping globalization that will eventually make everywhere uncannily similar to everywhere else?

Nevertheless, it is possible that architectural design may have something to learn from other 'designer' mass-production items, such as the Swatch watch, iMac and Porsche. Dutch architect Kas Oosterhuis has created a mass-production house strategy that utilizes the Internet as a design tool. It enables potential buyers to log on and create their own variation on a recognizably designed object called the Variomatic House. Oosterhuis maintains the 'Variomatic offers actual styling instead of selling architectural clichés'.[4] The theory is that you can buy into the designer label, but customize your own product, so each house (like different coloured/patterned/specification watches, computers and cars) is 'unique'.

The Los Angeles-based architect Wes Jones takes a different approach. He revels in consumerism icons and in his PRO/Con (PROgram/conTAINER) system he has used them not only as decorations but also as announcements to the neighbours of just what product you are signing up to.

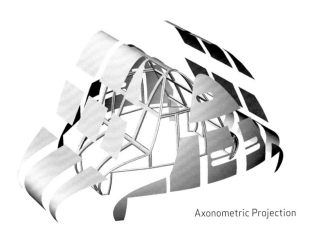

Axonometric Projection

PRO/Con Rooftop, Los Angeles, USA, 2004: Jones Partners.
This residence for a software developer based in San Francisco makes use of an 'undiscovered' rooftop landscape utilizing the services of its host building. The dwelling can turn through 360 degrees for completely flexible orientation.

PRO/Con is a system of building that uses standardized objects, combined with bespoke technological elements, to form the basis for a true architectural language, not just a style. The basic component is the standard ISO shipping container, which is used for its volumetric-form, low-cost and time-saving capacity. This is combined with a standardized, dedicated panel system that is constructed to the same module. Add to this gifted designers creating energetic, articulate, dedicated details, and a rich and varied architectural pattern book is created that can provide very individual buildings that respond both to the client and the site. Jones Partners have designed a wide range of buildings for sites across the USA in both urban and rural locations – these include single storey and multi-storey, family homes and apartment blocks. The houses are not just flexible in terms of the variations that can be achieved from the system, but also in terms of how they can be changed at will during use. The concept is based on the working parts being on show and on these adding to the understanding and operability of the architecture. Walls, stairs and floors not only *can* move, but they *need* to be moved because it is an important part of the building's character.

Modern houses, such as those Jones designs, are repeatedly used as the ideal location for the promotion of some other lifestyle 'essential', such as a car, fashion, food,

PRO/Con Rooftop, Los Angeles, USA, 2004: Jones Partners.

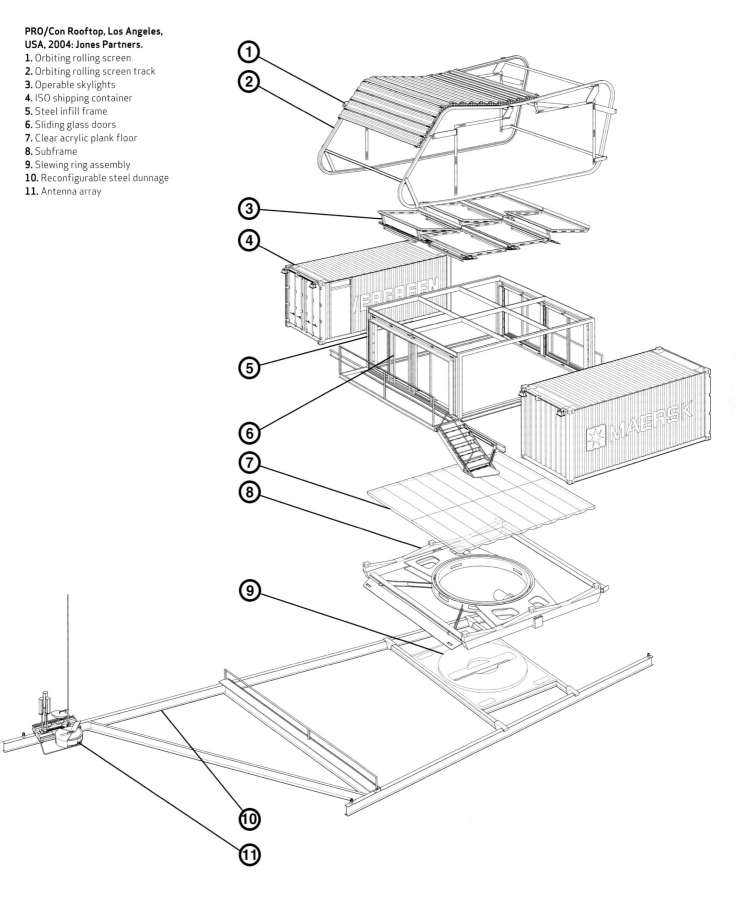

PRO/Con Rooftop, Los Angeles, USA, 2004: Jones Partners.

1. Orbiting rolling screen
2. Orbiting rolling screen track
3. Operable skylights
4. ISO shipping container
5. Steel infill frame
6. Sliding glass doors
7. Clear acrylic plank floor
8. Subframe
9. Slewing ring assembly
10. Reconfigurable steel dunnage
11. Antenna array

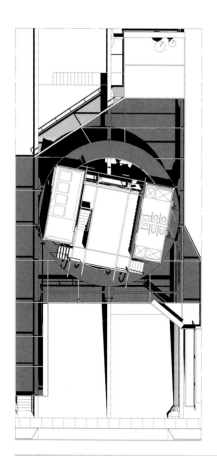

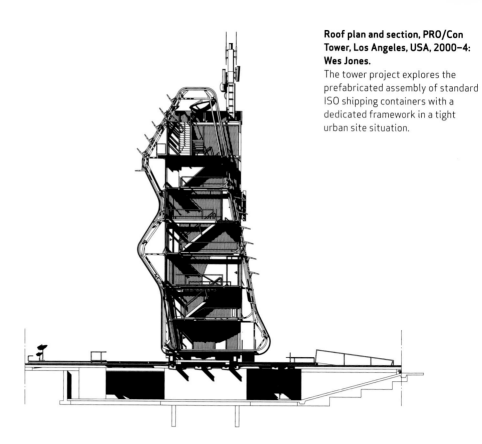

Roof plan and section, PRO/Con Tower, Los Angeles, USA, 2000–4: Wes Jones.
The tower project explores the prefabricated assembly of standard ISO shipping containers with a dedicated framework in a tight urban site situation.

PRO/Con Modular, Los Angeles, USA, 2000–4: Wes Jones.
PRO/Con package house systems are designed to provide economic yet individual dwellings in an age of high mobility, utilizing standard ISO shipping containers delivered by Skycrane helicopters.

drink, etc. Perhaps, therefore, the attachment of fashionable designer labels to the house itself is the inevitable next step. Jones has recognized this inextricable link that has led to the infinite and inadequate copies of retro pastiche as they have come in and out of style over centuries of home ownership. Jones' architecture is semi-industrial, dynamic and vigorous. His clients, who have commissioned him to build his current one-off house projects, have undoubtedly purchased the 'Jones' label, which represents contemporary innovation. Unfortunately, many others may choose to purchase Ralph Lauren or Martha Stewart styled 'house' containers, which instead utilize nostalgic remakes of past lives that in fact never existed.

The prefabricated building methods adopted by IKEA, Oosterhuis and Jones could provide the practical opportunity needed to build architecture that is not only flexible, but also costs as little as possible. In terms of housing there are many reasons why this is advantageous, besides the obvious one of making quality dwellings affordable for more people. Cheaper houses relinquish more resources for living and indulging in other experiences, consequently making economies more fluid instead of tying up capital in real estate. They encourage experimentation as less of a risk is being taken with the purchase, and their affordability makes them more likely to be the purchaser's first alternative rather than the more expensive and less innovative traditional building. One

Street view and roof plan, PRO/Con Ranch House, California, USA, 2000–5: Jones Partners.
This is a suburban house replacement proposal in which the vertical layering of the site is explored.

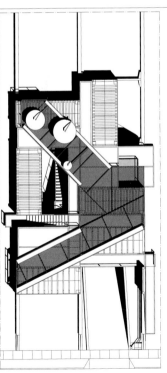

scenario could be a cheap house that can be recycled after a few years' use when a newer, more efficient and perhaps even cheaper one becomes available. This could lead to a rapid development in housing design as designers and manufacturers compete to be the market leader.

In terms of non-domestic architecture, commercially produced buildings that are designed within the principle of 'long-life: loose-fit' are already manifest in every aspect of the industry. Commercial, rentable-space office blocks are found in every city, and industrial and agricultural buildings are scattered everywhere else from technology parks to National Parks. The vast majority of these are bland at best, some are positively destructive of the environment in ecological terms and even more are damaging (and difficult to reverse) in their erosion of the regional character. Instead of this lowest common denominator architecture, where one size is created to fit all, architecture should be designed to be capable of being fine-tuned to fit each and every user in a specific way. In Open Building terms the flexibility can be varied depending on which level it is being created for – the infrastructure can be relatively fixed, the building frame stable but replaceable, the building skin easily revised and the internal partitions quickly relocated. In this way we can create architecture that relates to the place in which it is located, but still allows for significant change in its use.

Sub-'burb, California, USA, 2000: Jones Partners.

Sub-'burb, California, USA, 2000: Jones Partners.
This concept investigates a suburban housing model with twice the density of the norm but still providing a park-like upper surface from which the residents can benefit. Residents enter from the lower level, which also has courtyards and pools to create a cooling micro-climate.

Occupant-made shelters, Kamagawa River, Kyoto, Japan.

There is an even more radical way to envision a truly flexible architecture – where the building is considered separate from the plot that it occupies and is a facility rather than a property. Such a building may require the owner to relinquish the idea of an architecture that is inextricably linked with property and ownership of land. At first this sounds unreasonable – to change fundamentally the basis of our most significant financial investment. However, when the costs of relocating regularly are added up and fluctuations in the property market are considered, property ownership is not, perhaps, as good an investment as it once was. A lot of building accommodation is now rented, and cars, which we seem to have no trouble in accepting as a time-limited, non-sited possession, are our second most expensive owned item. So how about the idea of using sites that are in effect free? Think about all those millions of acres of roadsides, verges, empty inner-city building plots, ex-industrial land, and roofs. If these were accessible, serviced and open for use, then long-lasting but movable architecture would become viable.

In fact many of these places are used, though in ad-hoc and unofficial ways that are often invisible to most of society. In some cases so-called 'homeless' people reside there, 'so-called' because they obviously do have homes though to many they may seem wholly inadequate. Homeless persons' hand-crafted shelters are actually examples of

Tent City, Toronto, Canada, 2002:
Levitt Goodman.

non-professional, adaptable home building in the context
of the contemporary conditions of uncertainty and change.
Although they lack the basic conveniences that most of us
take for granted, when circumstances allow they are made
with care and ingenuity to create ephemeral, but invaluable,
living places for their residents.

Homeless people are not without possessions; they
have clothing, books, a radio, photographs – often the same
mementos that we all cling to. They also have the tools that
support their existence – bags, blankets, even a bicycle.
Perhaps their most significant portable object is the key that
unlocks their storage or shelter – a padlock can be a potent
symbol of both ownership and occupation. First Step
Housing, created by the Common Ground Community in New
York City, is an innovative project that uses the individual's
innate sense of home building to provide a pathway back
into a life away from the streets. Occupants can rent, for
a minimal fee, the basic building block of a home – a simple,
serviced space within an existing building shell that has
appropriate degrees of privacy and autonomy that they can
adopt and change as they desire. It reintroduces them to the
idea of being part of a community and having a recognizable
address that allows them access to benefits and employment.

There is an enormous inertia to overcome when
utilizing land to mitigate the problems of disenfranchised

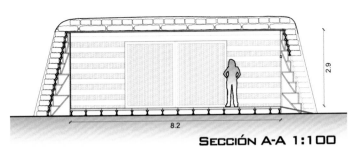

SECCIÓN A-A 1:100

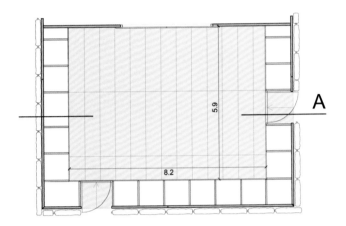

people. In 2002, Toronto architects Levitt Goodman became involved in creating a city government-sponsored response to the issue of 'homeless' appropriation of unused land, when they were invited to investigate how an urban area entitled 'Tent City' might be improved. Tent City was based on an area of brownfield land in an abandoned industrial district in south-east Toronto. The land was occupied by a core community of 175 residents, though this number increased significantly in the summer months. The residents had built their own makeshift homes from scrap materials, but land pollution and lack of running water meant living conditions were poor. In 2001, the homeless issue became politically charged, provoking action from the authorities. The proposal was to create a range of recyclable, temporary buildings and an infrastructure that would last for a maximum of three years – the time limit imposed by the city while alternative permanent accommodation was found. Just as a solution seemed to be within grasp, the city government lost its nerve and a number of obstructions were placed in the development's path, eventually resulting in its demise. 'Tent City' was bulldozed, a fence was erected around the site and residents were offered shelter in one of the city facilities or returned to the streets.[5]

The use of urban space is controlled by regulations that have been set up to protect cities and their inhabitants, and also to restrict non-conformist development and

Trincheras, Urban Prescriptions, Malaga, Spain, 2005: Santiago Cirugeda.
These art work spaces in Malaga were designed for self-build by students.

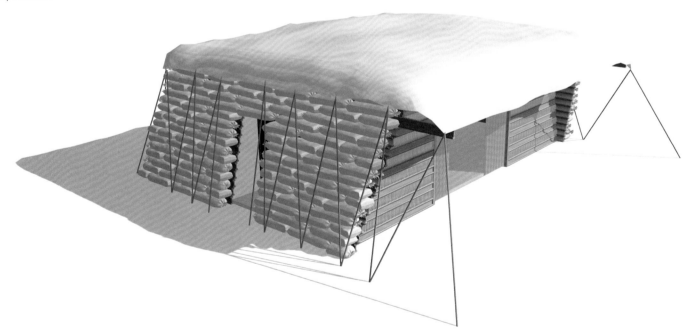

interaction. The designer and artist Santiago Cirugeda has developed strategies that subvert official legislation and control to enhance city living with informal development that ranges from the distinctly temporary to the transient and permanent. One of his strategies, Urban Refuge, is to use temporary licences to create more permanent installations – for instance obtaining a permit to erect scaffolding to do repairs or maintenance and then occupying the new structure as an addition to the building. Another is called Urban Reserves. This uses the permission granted to locate a building refuse container to create a public facility, for example a playground, a reading room, an information booth, an exhibition space or a performance venue. The structure superficially appears to be the container, but can be transformed into its new use on demand. Sensibly, he suggests that Urban Refuge constructors make the new structure themselves so that it looks like a commercial one but avoids confusion with any particular hire company. His most sophisticated projects have been temporary live and work spaces, built on a redundant plot of land and made possible by entering into a contract for water and electricity supply from a neighbour. The buildings are not legal but then again not strictly illegal either. The objective is not to take the land, but to use it temporarily while it would otherwise be unused.

Urban Prescriptions, Barcelona, Spain, 2005: Santiago Cirugeda.
This was a design for a small house erected on a vacant site in Barcelona.

Urban Refuge, Urban Prescriptions, Seville, Spain, 1998: Santiago Cirugeda.
House extension built on scaffolding.

Urban Prescriptions, Madrid, Spain, 2003–4: Santiago Cirugeda.
An Urban Prescriptions project under construction on a vacant site in Madrid – the structure uses standard components normally used for temporarily stabilizing façades and retaining walls. Plastic moulds designed for casting concrete drainage channels are used to make the façade.

Urban Prescriptions, Seville, Spain, 2004–5: Santiago Cirugeda.
Institutional Prosthesis is a live project, building prototype public work stations at the Contemporary Art Centre in Castelló, Spain.

Seattle houseboats, USA.

As well as the more or less sedentary, informal use of land and buildings there are those functions that habitually have a mobile existence. In dwelling terms these are the itinerant travellers: people who have chosen a life on the road in converted vehicles and towable trailers. Home for them is somewhere that is plugged into services as required, rather than as instructed. There are also other more socially acceptable forms of mobile living. The boat is a vehicle for communication, but the houseboat is a way of life that taps into the romantic connotations of travel to create a dwelling image with real mobile advantages. Many cities near water have a resident population moored alongside them, renting a place to park and a services connection rather than a piece of real estate. Though the houseboat has a traditional background, modern examples are likely to be as sophisticated in design and construction as comparable permanent dwellings.

The lakes of the Pacific Northwestern city of Seattle and the canals of the Netherlands have entire houseboat communities whose streets are duckboards or towpaths. New neighbours not only arrive with their possessions, but with the house as well. In the recent 'Parasite' (Prototypes for Advanced Ready-Made Amphibious Small-Scale Individual Temporary Ecological Houses) architectural project, devised by Mechthild Stuhlmacher and Rien Korteknie, a wide range of different responses to the problem of urban living were explored by the designers who took part. One interesting result was that rather than restricting the range of designs, the opportunity of building without a permanent site was actually an impetus to create innovative, yet realistic, proposals.[6] The new floating neighbourhood under construction in Ijburg was begun in 2000 and is due for completion in 2012. It is Amsterdam's new reclaimed city neighbourhood based on artificial islands close to the city centre – a rare example of an officially sponsored search for a typologically diverse urban housing pattern that will include 20 sites for Parasite dwellings.

Mobile buildings can be used in this ad-hoc way for other functions, in particular where the location is remote from governing authorities or the use is of a particularly short duration. Floating structures, such as oil rigs, fish-processing factory ships, laboratories, even a mobile airport, are used regularly in industry. These structures are understandably built to maritime standards so they must adhere to the regulations of their country of origin. Because they can be geographically located anywhere, however, there is a distinct informality about their operation when compared to a similar land-based operation. In a comparable situation, as long-distance passenger journeys have moved from ocean liners to airlines, passenger ships have been transformed from

North Sea oil rig, Cromarty, Scotland.

methods of transport into floating holiday complexes that can be operated on a more economic basis than land-based hotels by avoiding taxes and regulatory restrictions.

On land, mobile shops and markets that are set up to take advantage of a momentary event are the most commonplace form of commercial, ad-hoc land use. Though these group activities can grow into extensive events involving many thousands of people, they do not usually involve a substantial architectural component. The largest ad-hoc gatherings are probably associated with entertainment. Music concerts and festivals, though now much more of a commercial event than when they first began in the 1960s, in some cases still take place on a semi-formal basis, against the wishes of the authorities rather than with their blessing.

Lifestyle change is now becoming the norm rather than the exception. Home and work are becoming more about a set of activities than a specific geographic location. People are demanding more choice in not only how they live, but also where they live. Functional demands on public buildings are becoming more varied and more complex. Different ways of living and working are therefore resulting in the demand for buildings that must be flexible for ecological and economic reasons, as well as social and cultural ones. Architecture must fit the needs of its users better, be easier and more economic to operate and, when

Soba hut, Osaka, Japan. Sited on a busy intersection beneath a vehicle bridge, the hut's function is as an intimate restaurant for two or three people. It uses light-weight, natural bamboo screens to create a protected space, but also to advertise the nature of the activity the building contains.

Temporary café established beneath the InfoBox in Potsdamer Platz, Berlin. Conventional building forms and landscaping devices are used to establish a protected space.

change is necessary, avoid the waste associated with difficult demolition and rebuilding.

The contemporary designer's role, rather than creating a fixed setting for people's lives, can now be perceived as a sort of facilitator for the building user to create their own place that they can change as frequently as they wish. Instead of a fixed symbol of the taste and aspirations of the owner, the architecture becomes an indicator, though no more than that, of the meaning of the life and work that exists inside and also its possibilities for their future. Architecture still provides settings for the theatre of human existence, but these settings may now, if it is desired, be as variable as the occupants' moods or alternatively a fixed element in the changing pattern of living and working. Some changes may take place instantly, such as the switching on or off of an electric light dependent on the time of day or the mood desired while a book is read or a meeting takes place. Others may happen over months, years or even decades, depending on the changing nature and activities of the building's users.

Even in the conventional building there are some elements that are designed to be physically moved: doors, windows and roof lights; awnings and sunblinds; storage cupboards, closet doors and drawers. We are used to these movable elements in our buildings so without being too radical we can imagine (as many designers have)

needs and reinforce the family environment, making compatibility and continuity of shared space easier and more rewarding. For commerce and industry it should be a sustainable environment that adapts readily to changing economic conditions. For entertainment it should support a wide variety of changing shows for audiences and performers. For disaster relief it should be a responsive, supporting strategy that enables local people to direct their own needs.

Flexible architecture requires an attitude to design that integrates the requirements of the present with the possibility to adapt to changing situations in the future. It is not about predictive design (except in the sense that the prediction is that it will be different from the present), as predictions can be, and usually are, wrong. It is about allowing future users and designers, who will know their own situation best, the leeway to make appropriate decisions when they are needed. This can take the form of spaces and elements that are easily manipulated and altered on a day-to-day basis, or the capacity to be changed fundamentally with minimal disruption and expense as circumstances develop over a longer period. This does not mean that architects now need to focus on designing loose-fitting, non-dedicated environments without character. Instead the ambition should be to create buildings that have integrated, carefully devised systems that are capable of responding to new and varied situations. This

extrapolating the movement of these elements so that doors and windows become opening and closing walls; roof lights and awnings become opening and closing roofs; and cupboards and closets become moving rooms. Besides these physically operated, movable elements there are mechanical or electronic components that have also become integrated parts of the modern building with adjustable and movable features: heating, cooling and lighting services; safety, security and cleaning equipment; communication and leisure equipment; lifts for people and goods or equipment. We can also extrapolate how these elements might work if they were even more kinetic: a portable environmental unit that can be moved from space to space when needed with equipment, furniture and fittings that are stored away when not needed, rather than requiring a permanent room for their use; cleaning equipment that operates automatically at the place it is required; personal communications and entertainment that avoid duplication inside and outside the home; and instead of a single-use lift that is useless when it is not in use, why not have a whole room that rises and falls for the experience as well as the practical function?

A flexible building should be architecture that effervesces with the opportunities it offers to its users – an environment full of options and challenges that enhance the act and process of living. It should respond to individual

Concrete Canvas, London, UK, 2005: Peter Brewin and William Crawford. This emergency aid structure consists of a bag of cement-impregnated fabric. To erect the shelter just douse the bag with water and then inflate the bag to provide the temporary form-work. A few hours later the shell structure is ready for use.

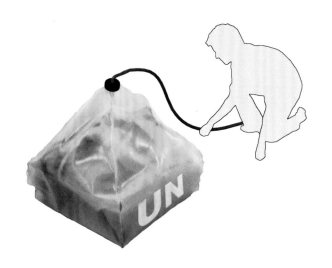

is architecture that needs designers' skills more than ever, not to create a product that is perfect on delivery (but destined for compromise in the future) but one that is capable of taking advantage of other contributors to the building's operation (most importantly the users) during its future lifetime. Flexible architecture, though it still may require the courage and persistence of individuals to see it through, is not arrogant or autocratic because it takes into account the fact that others have a say in the way buildings are made and used – flexible architecture is democratic.

Time and events are profound factors in shaping how well architecture is perceived and how it performs. Though architecture is an enduring aspect of human creativity, this factor should not result in a restrictive regime in its design. As Pierluigi Nicolin comments: 'In architecture the notion of time inevitably calls to mind the role of duration, usually assigned to monuments. Because of the aspiration to a condition of imperishability, architecture continues, in spite of everything, to seek … the utopia of a timeless dimension. As a result it seems to me that architects end up missing the opportunity to creatively include the temporal dimension of the event in architecture.'[7] The possibility of incorporating flexibility into the buildings we create, not just for now but also for the future, opens the opportunity genuinely to make buildings better and also to engage with events by providing them with a more meaningful setting that evolves over time.

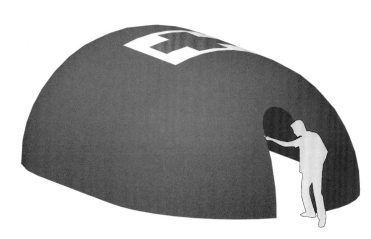

1 Reyner Banham, '1960 – Stocktaking' in *Architectural Review*, February 1960, vol.127, p.94. Banham developed these ideas further in his essay 'A Home is not a House', published in Charles Jencks and George Baird (eds.), *Meaning in Architecture*, New York, 1969, pp.109–18.
2 As quoted in Gevark Hartoonian, *Ontology of Construction: On Nihilism of Technology in Themes of Modern Architecture*, Cambridge, Mass., 1994, p.xiii.
3 See Nicolas Pope, *Experimental Houses*, London, 2000, pp.72–5.
4 Kas Oosterhuis and Ilona Lénard, 'Oosterhuis.nl' in *Archilab 2001*, Orléans, 2001, p.182.
5 See Dean Goodman, 'Mobile Architecture and Pre-manufactured Buildings: Two Case Studies' in Robert Kronenburg and Filiz Klassen (eds.), *Transportable Environments III*, London and New York, 2005.
6 See Mechthild Stuhlmacher and Rien Korteknie (eds), *The City of Small Things*, Rotterdam, 2001.
7 See Luca Ranconi, 'The Map of Action: A Conversation' in *Lotus International: Temporary*, no.122, November 2004.

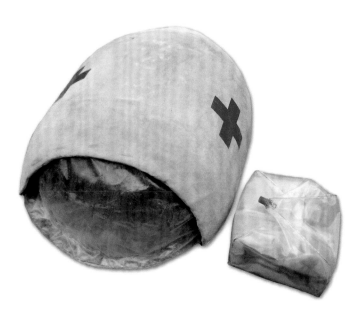

Part 2

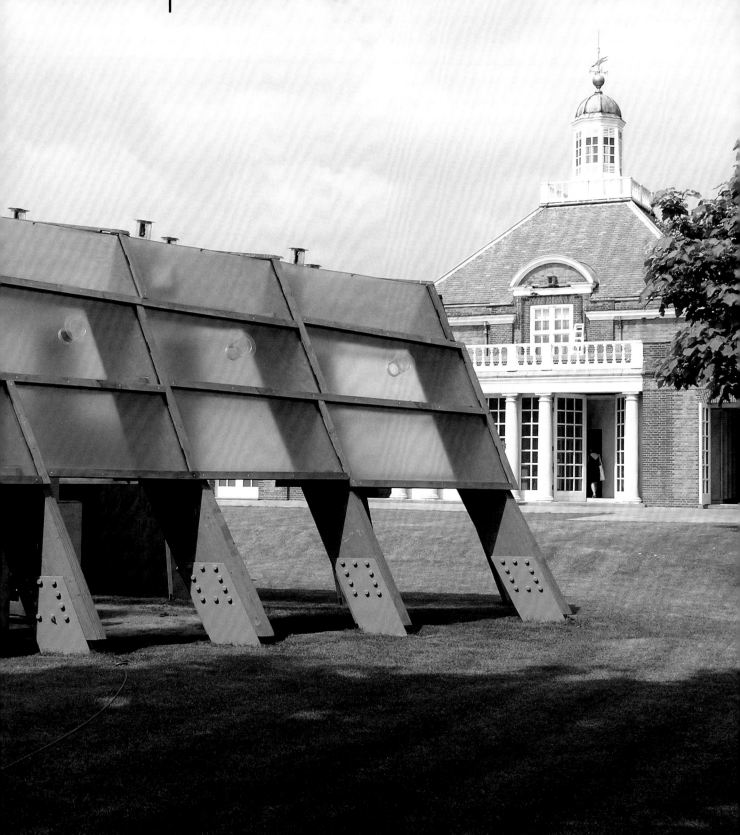

Adapt

Architecture that is designed for adaptation recognizes that the future is not finite, that change is inevitable, but that a framework is an important element in allowing that change to happen. Adaptable buildings are intended to respond readily to different functions, patterns of use and specific users' requirements, which is most easily seen in commercial developers' projects for office or retail premises. These are built with loose-fit space that can be fitted out as required by different designers and contractors as the main shell nears completion. This adaptability also means longer, more certain returns for the investor, as future change is easily accommodated within the fixed building fabric.

Serpentine Pavilion, London, UK, 2005: Álvaro Siza, Eduardo Souto de Moura and Cecil Balmond.

However, adaptable architecture is not just restricted to this overtly commercial response. The use of an adaptable design strategy recognizes that the building delivery process is not always something that is undertaken by a single individual or team to create a fixed object, but is a process of collaboration between a range of participants. It also builds in the capacity for these different participants to interact with the design process at different times in the building's history, thereby allowing change to be a continuous, ongoing process. There is no doubt that great architecture can result from a single vision, encompassing every aspect of the design from the urban vision to the interior furniture and fittings. The *Gesamtkunstwerk* (the complete work of art) is an important part of architectural achievement. However, great buildings still need to retain relevance and usefulness as time passes and circumstances change, so different participants in the creative process, who are tuned into current needs, must be allowed to take part and make contributions.

Adaptable architecture also allows for the easy introduction of new technologies that are improvements on those that were initially installed in the building. The complete rebuilding of architecture as technological change occurs is neither efficient nor desirable. Changes in services, communications and security needs are inevitable and should be allowed to happen incrementally so that previous systems can interface with new ones. Allowing flexible conduits for these systems not only allows for replacement and upgrading, but also for planning layout and functional space changes.

Perhaps the most significant attribute of adaptable architecture is that it allows the users of the building to influence design decisions. Because the building plan has more capacity for different layouts, both at its inception and when change occurs in the future, clients, users and inhabitants are able to get closer to their needs because there are fewer restrictions fixed in place by the shell designer. Not only can they choose their own designer to create the space they need, the designer has greater freedom in creating that space.

The most formalized strategy for adaptable architectural design is the Open Building principle, which designates distinct levels of intervention in the built environment that range from urban design at a city scale to the individual fit-out of rooms and spaces. Design work should be done at each level with reference to the next, but the resultant built intervention should not be so fixed as to restrict flexibility when change occurs.

In the example of a developer-led retail project, the developer and their design and construction team work at the base building level while the shop owners and their design and construction team work at the fit-out level.

Amsterdam Arts Metropole

The Netherlands, project 2005: Weil Arets

This conversion of a 1970s, six-storey office block is a venue for contemporary arts where any sort of installation or performance might be expected. The internal spaces are entirely column free for extra flexibility. This is made possible by a steel lattice structure on the perimeter incorporating a double skin that includes all services and circulation. The façade shifts in appearance from an obscure screen to a transparent window, depending on the perspective from which it is viewed.

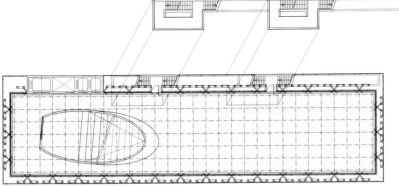

Lecture Level Floor Plan

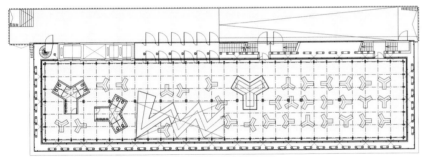

Entrance Level Floor Plan

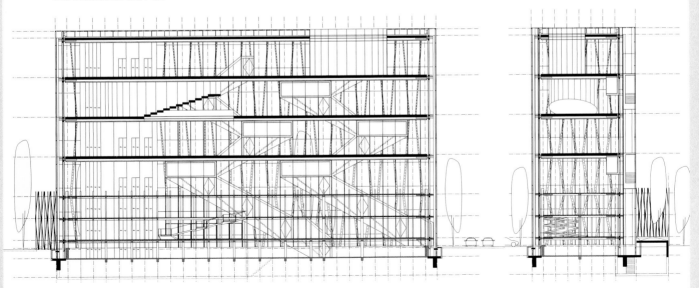

Sections

This distinction between the different levels of intervention creates a built-in framework for flexibility, in that there are recognizable interfaces where the change can occur with minimum disruption to the level above.

Though there are many buildings that have been built using Open Building principles, perhaps the most complex is the INO addition to the Insel University Hospital campus in Bern, Switzerland. After years of attempting to fix a programme for the new facility, which was thwarted by constant changes in staff, space, equipment and operational requirements, a new planning process was adopted that prioritized adaptability instead of programme. The INO project was therefore split into three systems, each dependent on its operational life span: primary system – up to 100 years; secondary system – up to 20 years; tertiary system – up to 10 years. After limited competitions, teams of designers and managers were selected for each of the three levels, together with Bern-based Suter + Partner Architekten ('team 0') who were designated as co-ordinators and managers. The primary system, or 'base building', was designed by Peter Kamm and Kundig Architects on an 8.4 metre (27.6 foot) grid with the provision for vertical circulation and service points provided in each bay in a 3.6 metre (11.8 foot) 'punch-through' zone. The design of the secondary system was based on existing hospital use, but

INO hospital addition, Bern,
Switzerland, 2001– :
Suter + Partner Architekten.

Adapt

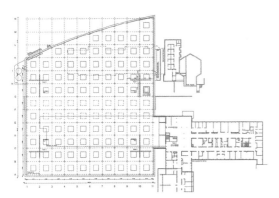

Primary system layout

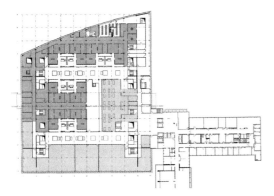

Cluster layout

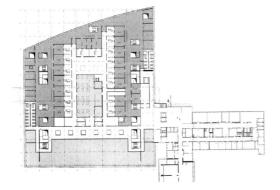

Linear layout

INO hospital addition, Bern,
Switzerland, 2001– :
Suter + Partner Architekten.

using many different possible scenarios so the building could be utilized in many different ways in the future, either by refitting rooms, changing equipment and systems or by changing partitions and surfaces. Appropriately high levels of servicing allow quick replacement of outdated machinery and equipment for optimum performance and multi-functionality of spaces for the tertiary system. The project is operational in 2006 and is the subject of a long-term study by the Building Futures Institute at Ball State University, Indiana, USA.

The simplest strategy that can be used to provide adaptable buildings might at first seem to be the provision of multi-use space – rooms and places that can accommodate a wide range of functions. Architecture is replete with rooms that can do just this: meeting rooms that become teaching rooms in schools; black-box theatres that can support different sorts of performances and audience configurations; and hotel conference suites that become wedding, exhibition and show venues. However, multi-uses spaces, if they are to work effectively in their different functions, are complex design problems. Air quality, movement, and temperature; lighting, black-out and projection; food and drink provision; means of escape and security – these are some of the critical factors that demand a large investment in a complex servicing system. This often leads to multi-use spaces becoming bland, enclosed volumes without architectural character or personality.

Schaulager (Art Store)

Basel, Switzerland, 2004: Herzog and De Meuron

The Schaulager is essentially a new building type: part gallery, part warehouse and part education facility. The name means a 'display warehouse' where art is stored in curated display cells enabling continuous conservation and access by scholars. The building has an auditorium, café and bookshop, and an exhibition area. Above this are three levels of flexible space with 11,500 square metres (123,800 square foot) of independently controlled display/storage cells.

This does not always have to be the case. Since 2000 the Serpentine Gallery in Kensington Gardens, London, UK has each year commissioned an internationally acclaimed architect to design a temporary pavilion that is sited on its lawn during the summer months – Zaha Hadid (2000), Daniel Libeskind and Arup (2001), Toyo Ito and Arup (2002), Oscar Niemeyer (2003), MVRDV (2004). The building has a multi-purpose function, as a coffee shop in the day and a space for lectures, meetings and entertainment in the evening. This brief remains constant, as does the site; however, the range of variations in response to how the site is used and the form of the building is dramatically diverse. The fact that this is a temporary pavilion (though each building has subsequently been made available for re-siting as a more permanent structure) provides the designers with freedom to seek expression for its loose function and also to respond to external factors that engage with experimental design concerns.

The 2005 Serpentine Pavilion was the result of a collaboration between Álvaro Siza, Eduardo Souto de Moura and Arup engineer Cecil Balmond. The building consisted of a distorted rectangular wooden grid that formed a curving dome supported on slanting grid walls on four sides. Though the principal wooden members were straight, the primary impression was of a bending, tensioned structure crouching on the ground. Translucent polycarbonate panels provided gentle

Serpentine Pavilion, London, UK, 2005: Álvaro Siza, Eduardo Souto de Moura and Cecil Balmond.

Adapt

Serpentine Pavilion, London, UK,
2005: Álvaro Siza, Eduardo Souto
de Moura and Cecil Balmond.

Yokohama Ferry Terminal, Japan,
2002: Foreign Office Architects.

filtering of the light during the daytime. At night, a solar-powered lamp at the centre of each panel provided a very different ambience. The building was open to the elements at the perimeter, but once inside it felt very much like a contained space. Loose, light, movable furniture, designed by Siza, complemented the impression of a space that was ephemeral and changeable.

A very different multi-use project, built on a much larger scale and with a different agenda, is the Yokohama Ferry Terminal by Farshid Moussavi and Alejandro Zaera Polo of the UK architectural practice Foreign Office Architects. The result of a competition win in 1994, the terminal was completed in 2002. Yokohama is a city close to Tokyo and is the most important port access for Tokyo and consequently Japan. The terminal has a primary function as a pier, which provides direct access for passengers to cruise ships; it also has other roles that create a complex programme that the architects have interpreted in an intuitive yet ingenious way. The steel-frame building projects out into the bay and consists of a multi-level structure with separate pedestrian and vehicle movement zones. The top deck is a remarkable shifting ground plane, a timber-clad pier that undulates to create an artificial landscape that is an extension of the city's Yamashita Park and consequently of the city itself. The client instigated this strategy by introducing the concept of *Ni-wa-minato*,

Yokohama Ferry Terminal, Japan, 2002: Foreign Office Architects.

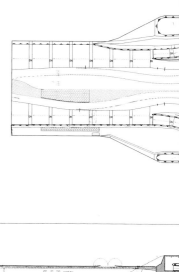

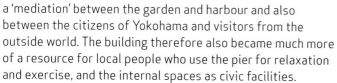

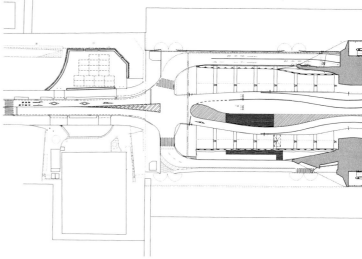

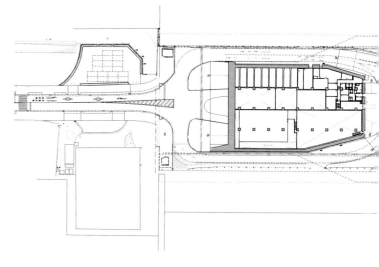

a 'mediation' between the garden and harbour and also between the citizens of Yokohama and visitors from the outside world. The building therefore also became much more of a resource for local people who use the pier for relaxation and exercise, and the internal spaces as civic facilities.

    The terminal's interior levels are 'pleated' to guide pedestrian and vehicle traffic into routes that serve the loading of the ships. Circulation is complex because of the large capacity of the ships, their conflicting schedules and their different national and international destinations. FOA describe this as a planning 'battleground', but they have solved this need for flexibility by creating large, open spaces that can be redefined with mobile and collapsible barriers and surveillance points to reconfigure the boundaries between territories. They also wished to undermine the typical sense of a gateway that occurs at departure points, making transition for the passengers easier – from city to public park to transportation. The architects believe that the Yokohama Ferry Terminal is a functional response to a problem concerning a sense of displacement characteristic in our age. By addressing the mobile habitation of the ground as a shifting entity it becomes symbolic of this issue. They used the very different ground plane they have designed as a connecting device that not only physically brings together the city and the sea, but also draws its inhabitants to the defining edge where the two meet.

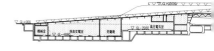

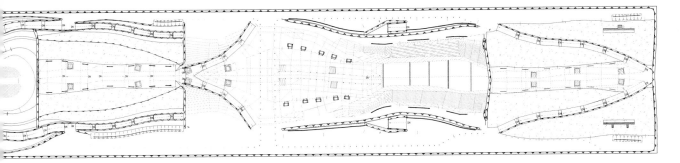

Second Level

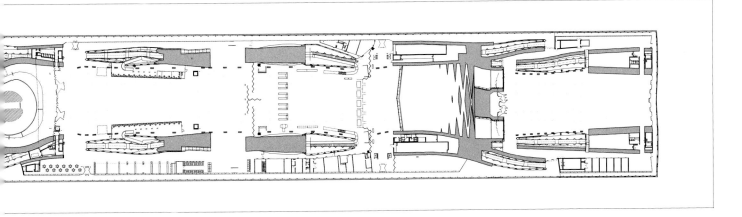

First Level

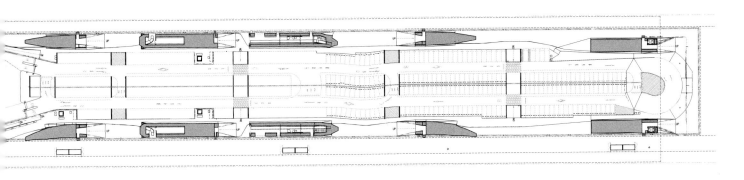

Ground Level

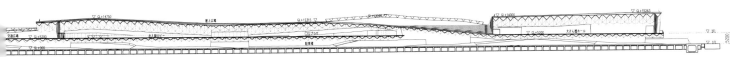

Long Section

Adapt

Yokohama Ferry Terminal, Japan, 2002: Foreign Office Architects.

A valid criticism of adaptable space is that it cannot provide a close fit to the functions that it must support. It is a solution that must, by necessity, be able to accommodate other uses and these may be compromised. A strategy that deals with this issue is the idea of fluctuating space. In essence this approach to design is to incorporate in a building dedicated, functional spaces that address specific functions that need to be carried out there, but are also directly linked with more ambiguous territory – a sort of buffer zone in which many things can happen. This allows the dedicated space to be appropriately serviced, decorated and furnished, but also allows unplanned, ad-hoc activities to expand out from it as required. A typical example might be the traditional proscenium arch theatre, which has an auditorium with fixed tiered seating at several levels with direct aspect towards the stage. This is complemented by two separate buffer zones: the backstage area and the lobby. The backstage area is often very large, allowing for a wide variety of different types of performance and also for scenery, hidden backstage performance by musicians and cross-stage access during shows. This area often extends high above the auditorium for flying backdrops and has direct access to the outside for the delivery of scenery and props. The lobby allows space for the whole audience to leave quickly and also often has space set aside for a box office, sale of programmes, a bar and even a

Seattle Public Library, USA, 2004:
Rem Koolhaas OMA.

restaurant. Many theatres also have front of house informal performances or exhibitions.

This concept of fluctuating space was used by Rem Koolhaas and the Office for Metropolitan Architecture in their design for the Seattle Public Library, USA completed in 2004. Koolhaus feels that libraries as a building type have become increasingly compromised by the multitude of tasks they must now undertake in comparison to their traditional role as a book-based resource. Their need to be information stores that respond to all aspects of media has resulted in bland, open-plan floors that allow the flexibility of shifting demands, but also lead to spaces defined by book-stacks and computer terminals. The approach taken with the Seattle Public Library was to create a series of spatial compartments, each dedicated to a specific role. Each compartment would have tailored flexibility within it to respond to its own specific needs, but it would not also have to deal with the problems arising from different functions.

This led to a building concept with a series of floors of different character, each closely designed to fulfil its own function. The spaces between the floors became interfaces where a variety of work, relaxation and entertainment functions could operate and trade off the interaction between the activities on either side. This interactivity is underlined at the beginning of the visitor's experience of

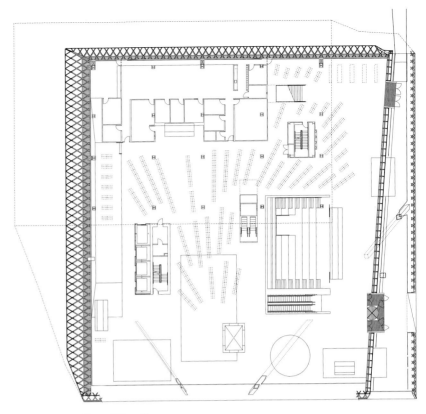

Ground Floor Plan

**Seattle Public Library, USA, 2004:
Rem Koolhaas OMA.**

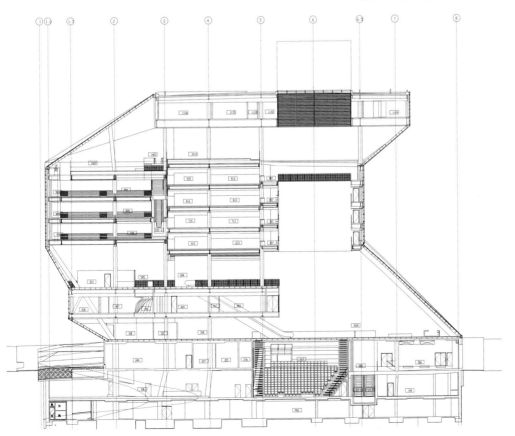

Section

the building in the Mixing Chamber. This is an area where librarians and users have maximum contact, with access to all the information sources in the library. Flexibility for the ever-increasing mass of information that libraries have to accrue was addressed in the design of the 'book spiral'. This runs continuously through four floors and contains all the library's non-fiction books. Its purpose is to allow the collection to increase progressively (rather than breaking it up for restacking as it exceeds its allotted space).

The need simply to *build*, as a symbol of a city's changing status and a physical sign of its regeneration, has spawned many new buildings. The building type is more often than not a museum or exhibition space – a function that can be justified as having value both for locals and potential new visitors and investors in the city's future. In the early twenty-first century, Manchester in the UK invested in three new museum projects including work by Daniel Libeskind and Michael Hopkins. Its third project was the result of an international competition held in 1998 and won by local designer, Ian Simpson. The initial proposals for Urbis, a museum of the modern city, were generic because the exact function of the building had yet to be decided. Indeed it was only in the year before its completion in 2002 that a management company was appointed.

The building was designed as an urban 'fixer' that would redefine public space and instigate new investment

**Urbis, Manchester, UK, 2000–2:
Ian Simpson.**

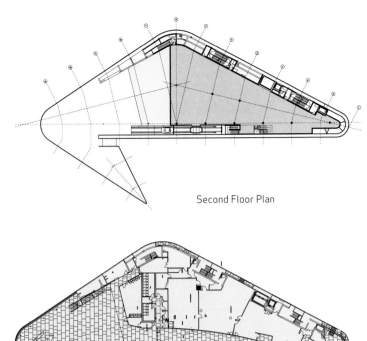

Second Floor Plan

Ground Floor Plan

in a previously disregarded area of the city, while providing a venue for a public exhibition of mutable substance. Simpson created a remarkable iconic structure – a shining glass wedge, set in a high-quality urban garden with a curving prow that responds to the curves in the nineteenth-century stone façades in the city centre. Although it is six storeys high, the space is largely continuous and served by a funicular lift that not only takes you to the top of the building with its stunning views of the city, but also allows you to preview the physical shape of the installations on each floor. Unfortunately, the initial exhibitions have been disappointing. The ostensibly interactive displays that communicate the character of the urban situation around the world are in the main either simplistic or confusing and typically turn their back on the quality of the grand interconnecting interior space that has been created to host them. However, the space is designed to accommodate change – the simple, triangular, open floor plates are framed on one side by service spaces and escape stairs, on another by the funicular and views of the city and on the third by the open space of the building itself with a continuous roof light that provides views over the roofscape.

In order to work, these adaptable design strategies – layered design, multi-use space and fluctuating space – need to utilize appropriate constructional and operational systems. These can vary significantly depending on the

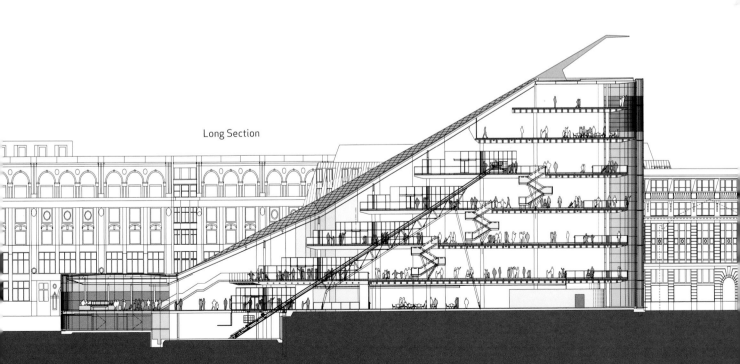

Long Section

Barn Operating Theatre

Liverpool, UK, 2005: Nightingale Associates

This operating theatre at Broadgreen Hospital in Liverpool combines four surgical teams in a single large room with shared preparation and cleaning facilities. This allows greater flexibility in performing operations and better opportunities for teaching, with expert advice available from an adjacent non-sterile area. Theatre walls are modular stainless-steel panels that can be removed to allow replacement of equipment as it becomes obsolete. Pressurized air systems above each table prohibit the chance of cross-infection.

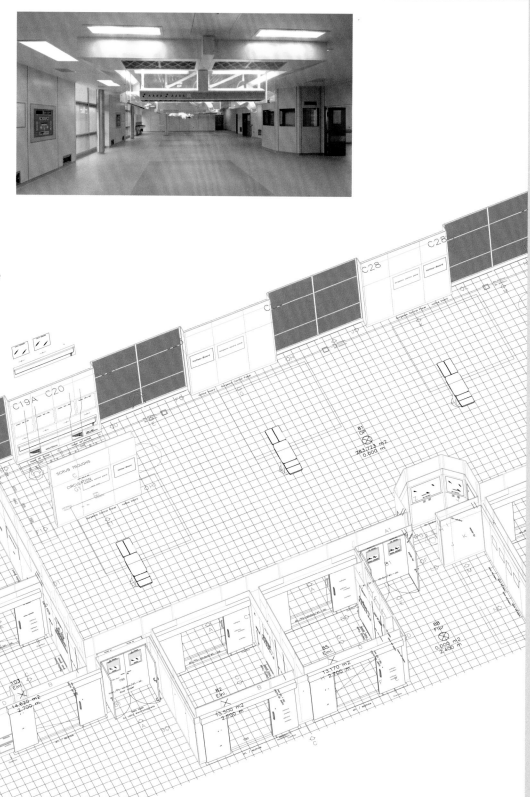

Centre Pompidou

Metz, France, 2004–7: Shigeru Ban

The commission for this new arts centre is strategically located on the Germany, Belgium and Luxembourg border and results from a competition win. Shigeru Ban and collaborators Jean de Gastines and Philip Gumuchdjian have designed a vast modular, hexagonal, latticed steel and wood structure, clad in a translucent fibreglass membrane. This covers the entire complex including exhibition, public and administrative facilities, which are located in shiny, metal-clad, rectangular tubes. The roofs are usable, sheltered surfaces, as are the spaces below the exhibition galleries. The informal organic 'tent-like' structure contrasts with the elevated 'buildings', blurring the boundaries between the building's different functions and also between outside and inside.

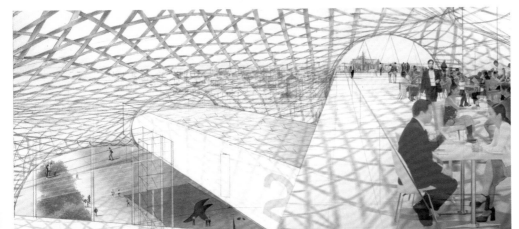

complexity and nature of the function, but there are two principal areas that have a fundamental effect on the flexibility of the building – prefabricated modular constructional systems and adaptive servicing.

Particularly in housing, but also in some other areas of architectural design, prefabrication is seen as a route towards greater efficiency and faster provision. In several countries, for example Acorn Houses in the USA, Huf Haus in Germany and BoKlok in Sweden, factory-made housing has been introduced extremely successfully. It is a way of solving the need for the delivery of improved construction standards and increased demand in the face of a lack of skilled site labour, small and restrictive sites and a competitive market. A modular approach to design and construction has also led to much more adaptable buildings that are able to respond to their users' needs and desires.

Japan has some of the most sophisticated widespread modular house building systems. Companies like Toyota and Sekisui have developed a system where houses are designed in close interaction with clients. A special computer programme itemizes all the components as the clients collaborate with a company designer/salesperson to make their choice. This gives an accurate feedback on what the house will be like and what it will cost. As with other prefabricated systems, there are many variations in materials

Prefabricated modular houses, Kobe, Japan.

UK Millennium Experience Dome

London, UK, 1999: Richard Rogers and Buro Happold

Designed with Buro Happold, Rogers' Millennium Dome defied the original brief from the British Government, which was to create a series of independent 'experience' pavilions, in order to provide an adaptable building capable of re-use after the Millennium celebrations were over. Though widely criticized for the internal exhibits, the building itself was generally regarded as an engineering success, built to last a minimum of 20 years and capable of relocation if necessary. It will be adapted to provide a gymnasium and basketball centre for the London Olympics in 2012, and for use by local residents beyond that as a sports and entertainment complex.

and finishes, but instead of choosing from a set of basic house plans the layout and style of the building are also infinitely variable, within the restriction of the standardized components that can be both flat-pack and volumetric modules. When the design is set, the order is transmitted to the factory and preparation of the components begins – in Sekisui's case this is on their 400 metre (1,312 foot) long assembly line. Components are packaged up and loaded onto delivery vehicles in a 'just-in-time' system that avoids storage on site.

This method of building can lead to a dramatically different urban pattern. After the 1995 Hanshin-Awaji earthquake large areas of the city of Kobe were destroyed. This was mostly due to the ensuing fire, which could not be extinguished due to broken water mains and the narrow street pattern that restricted access for emergency vehicles. Consequently, a new urban design layout was quickly designed by the city authorities that would help prevent a similar disaster occurring. Residents were allocated new building plots on, or close by, their old houses. Many of the new houses were built using the new factory-made system and an incredibly diverse neighbourhood has resulted: eclectic and informal, many would say un-designed and even kitsch, but also highly personal and responsive to those who live there.

Optima Homes, UK, 2004: Cartwright Pickard and Pace Timber Systems.

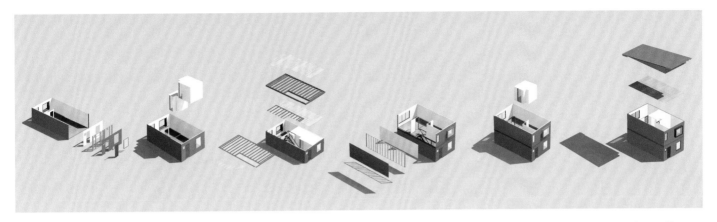

Assembly sequence, Optima Homes, UK, 2004: Cartwright Pickard and Pace Timber Systems.

Much attention has been given recently to the potential for off-site production methods to improve the delivery of affordable housing in the UK. One new product that has been developed in response to this need, but also aims to make a significant improvement in client choice and adaptability, is Optima Homes, designed by Cartwright Pickard in collaboration with timber frame manufacturers Pace Timber Systems. The system is directed specifically towards terraced and semi-detached houses, though it has the potential to deliver flats up to five storeys high. It consists of a closed wall panel system that is delivered to site complete with dry-lining, insulation, conduits, external walls and windows pre-installed in the factory in co-ordination with kitchen and bathroom pods that incorporate components and services pre-fitted for easy connection. House builders, designers and clients can use the components either as part of a standard plan from the Optima range, or customize them into a completely unique solution.

A fundamental feature of adaptable design is the requirement to have equally adaptable servicing. In multi-use spaces the services need to be tuned in different ways so that they can respond to the functions that are being supported at any one time. This principally means changes in lighting, heating and air movement, but also power and communications systems supply, security, fire alarms and

means of escape. Such spaces may also be capable of sub-division and re-zoning, so the control systems have to be sufficiently sophisticated to allow for this. These requirements mean that such a servicing system is complex and expensive but it also means that it is able to accommodate rapid change, even enabling many different uses within a single day. Longer-term change is just as important, particularly when it comes to housing where flexibility is necessary either as a family's needs develop over time or when new residents move in. In both cases the house layout should be able to adapt to new lifestyles. For example, in family housing a couple may have children, then the children grow older and leave home. In elderly persons' housing a resident may become less mobile as they grow older. Clearly, it is desirable that significant changes to the plan should be possible to accommodate varying lifestyles.

Dutch architect Frans van der Werf has advocated adaptable design since the 1970s and has constructed several award-winning housing projects that utilize sustainable construction. His Pelgromhof project in Zevenaar in the Netherlands was begun in 1997, completed in 2001 and provides accommodation for 169 residents. It has a projected minimum flexible life cycle of 75 years (compared to the usual 50 years for this type of project). The entire complex is built using sustainable materials in a courtyard form that

Pelgromhof, Zevenaar, the Netherlands, 1997–2001: Frans van der Werf.

integrates the natural landscape with a compact, energy-efficient plan. The individual apartments are built using a flexible servicing system that allows residents to design their own apartments according to their needs and tastes. The housing is intended for people aged 50 and over and is designed on the principle of 'lifetime guaranteed dwelling' that responds to the residents' needs at different stages in their life, for example if mobility or visibility is impaired at some point.

Such flexible servicing systems can also be retrofitted to existing buildings to extend their life. The Matura system was fitted into another Dutch housing scheme at Prinses Beatrixlaan in Voorburg by architect Reijenga Postma Hagg beginning in 1989, 30 years after it was first built. Existing residents were able to completely redesign their apartment layout, move into temporary accommodation and return one month later to their new homes. A team of just three workmen moved from dwelling to dwelling within the block installing the new services systems until the entire project was complete. Research into the continuing benefits of this flexible renovation process for subsequent and future change is still ongoing.

The principle of a loose-fit space that can accommodate a wide range of uses is a fundamental building form that is found from the very beginning of architectural history. This multi-purpose space building type can be found

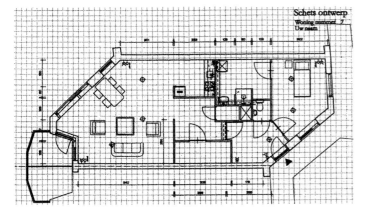

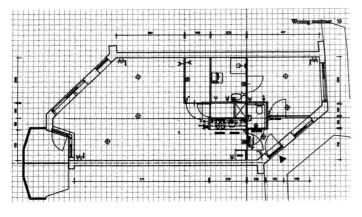

Pelgromhof, Zevenaar, the Netherlands, 1997–2001: Frans van der Werf.

Rijnwaarden te Tolkamer

The Netherlands, 2003–5:
Frans van der Werf

This recent housing project continues Frans van der Werf's commitment to sustainable building in terms of materials and energy use. It also includes flexible apartments for residents that feature lifetime residency guarantees because of the ability of the layouts to accommodate accessibility changes when required.

in both agricultural (the barn or grange) and residential (hall) settings. In industry the large, open-plan space that accommodates machines of different types, powered from a unified source, is an archetype that emerges directly from the Industrial Revolution, when multi-storey mill buildings were situated first near to water-power sources and then in urban centres as coal-driven steam power became available.

Contemporary industrial buildings take this form to allow for changes in the production-line process as manufacturers respond to new product demands or the introduction of new machinery and processes. The Igus® factory in Cologne, Germany has been built for even greater flexibility than usual. Igus® is a family-owned business that makes injection-moulding tools – technologically innovative components that were previously made of metal. The tools differ widely depending on the task they are required to do and consequently the company has developed a very flexible approach to production by changing the process frequently to increase efficiency.

Nicholas Grimshaw and Partners have designed the company's current factory (completed in 2001), which was developed over a period of more than a decade. The design team developed a modular building system that allows a column-free space and easy relocation of building elements and components. The plan consists of a series of 68 metre

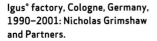

Igus® factory, Cologne, Germany, 1990–2001: Nicholas Grimshaw and Partners.

(223 foot) wide, square bays with a roof that is suspended from a tall pylon. The cladding is a demountable, aluminium panel system that uses dry fixing throughout to allow individual panels or whole walls to be changed or relocated. The administration and office facilities are provided in pods that are elevated on steel legs with flat, disc-like feet. These can also be moved around to any location within the factory by lifting them onto air-supported, scene-shifting trolleys that are usually used in the theatre. The pods are then pushed by forklift truck to another location where one of the many service points is positioned.

Adaptable architecture is necessary where more complex building types must respond to change. It is particularly valuable in housing where a more tuned response to the needs of the user is beneficial in improving their quality of life. It is also of value in building types that have unpredictable or varied functions – exhibitions, education, medicine, entertainment, factory production and warehousing. Adaptable buildings tend to have a higher servicing element than fixed-use solutions, and so can be more expensive when first constructed. Despite this, they have the benefit of being able to fulfil their function better and to have an extended life. Adaptability, therefore, has the additional advantage of being a key strategy in providing a sustainable building solution as well as an appropriate one.

Igus® factory, Cologne, Germany,
1990–2001: Nicholas Grimshaw
and Partners.

Transform

Glass Shutter House, Tokyo, Japan, 2004: Shigeru Ban.

All buildings have operational features. Doors open, windows sometimes do. Much of a building's furniture is also movable and, even though the architect may have designed an optimum placing, it can usually be repositioned. Furnishings, such as blinds and curtains, can change the lighting of a space. In general, furniture and furnishings are the most usual user-customizable components in building design and they can, without doubt, dramatically alter the appearance and ambience of a space. However, in order fundamentally to change the way that a building can be used, more significant alterations are required and in conventional buildings this cannot take place without significant constructional intervention.

Bengt Sjostrom Starlight Theater, Rockford, Illinois, USA, 2003: Studio Gang O'Donnell (now Studio Gang Architects).

Truly transformable architecture must go far beyond the minimal changes allowed by moving the chairs around or painting the walls. It must enable a dramatic alteration in the character of the whole architectural environment. A transformable building is therefore one that changes shape, volume, form or appearance by the physical alteration of structure, skin or internal surface, enabling a significant alteration in the way it is used or perceived. This is architecture that opens, closes, expands or contracts. Transformation of this kind is not an easy characteristic to introduce into building. Kinetic, constructional elements that are capable of relocating on a regular basis require far greater design and manufacturing effort. Problems occur in three main areas: movement mechanisms; joining of internal and external partitions; and operation of services under the different conditions.

The mechanisms employed to enable movement to take place should be robust, maintenance free, easily operable and reliable. In some cases, particularly in domestic situations, this means the building should be capable of transformation with human power alone. This simple, physical act can not only alter the space, but also increase the user's connection with the building and its changing environment. For larger alterations this is not feasible, even in the domestic situation, so power-operated devices are required.

Bengt Sjostrom Starlight Theater, Rockford, Illinois, USA, 2003: Studio Gang O'Donnell (now Studio Gang Architects).

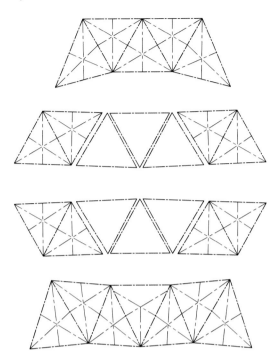

Roof geometry showing fixed and movable elements

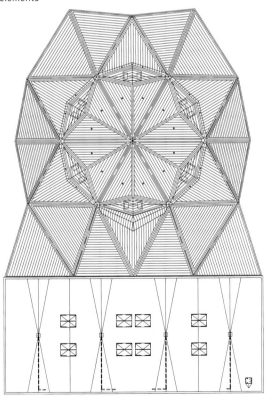

There is something magical about this act – a building becoming kinetic at the touch of a button can introduce a potent reinvention of something inanimate, giving it the quality of being alive. It is vital that power-operated roofs, walls and doors are completely reliable so that they can close instantly when required; for this reason, extremely well-tested electric, hydraulic or pneumatic mechanisms are essential. Safety systems are also an important part of power-operated mechanisms, ensuring that they stop automatically if there is a fault or if an emergency occurs.

Another aspect of mechanical movement of building parts is that opening and closing joints must occur. When the opening partition is external this can lead to weather-proofing issues. Correct detailing of fixed joints is a well-understood practice; however, it is not unknown for new buildings to leak as a result of faulty workmanship or materials or the introduction of unforeseen circumstances at the design stage. Therefore, the detailing of a kinetic joint with at least two completely different states of existence is a much more complex task. New materials have made this job easier, with the introduction of plastics such as neoprene that maintain their flexibility and integrity over much longer periods. Strategies employed in other industries, particularly vehicle design, can also prove valuable precedents in solving problems in this area.

Internal transformation also presents fresh problems. A critical issue is air transmission between the divided spaces. Acoustic separation will usually be required to enable them effectively to operate independently, but fire separation is even more critical as safety is at risk if this fails to work as planned. A less critical issue, but still an important one if the building is to provide uncompromised service, is that the finishes in the movement area should not be marked or damaged by the transitional operation. An important part of the success of transformable buildings is that the service they deliver in all their different states is at least as good as the service static structures deliver.

Building services designed for transformable spaces must operate effectively in a much wider range of circumstances than conventional buildings. Though there are seasonal variations in all climates, these usually take place over a longer period of time. For example, a building that can open its entire roof might suddenly experience much higher humidity levels while it is open, which will have to be dealt with quickly when the roof is closed so that internal finishes are not damaged. Heating, cooling and ventilation may therefore require much faster response times than conventional buildings. In addition, provision of services may be restricted because it is not feasible to place cable or duct runs in moving partitions or surfaces. In spaces that are

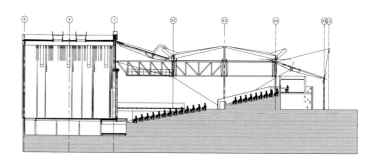

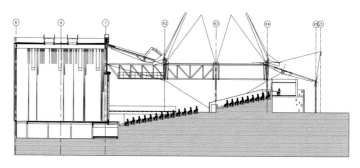

Sections showing roof open and closed

Bengt Sjostrom/Starlight Theater, Rockford, Illinois, USA, 2003: Studio Gang O'Donnell (now Studio Gang Architects).

divided, lighting or communication points have to be carefully designed to operate effectively when different configurations are in place. Controls for all services may have to have multiple operating modes and points of access for the same reason.

Transformable architecture also places an important additional aspect of environment control within the power of the building user. A critical reason for the introduction of transformation is to enable buildings to engage with the external environment and thereby to respond to external climatic conditions. A glass wall that enables separation from the outside in inclement weather can be removed when conditions allow, breaking the formal barrier that buildings usually have between the inside and outside. Similarly, a roof can be opened to enhance the connection to light and sky for atmospheric or environmental reasons. The Bengt Sjostrom/Starlight Theater was designed by Studio Gang O'Donnell (now Studio Gang Architects) for Rock Valley College in Illinois, USA, and completed in 2003. The building replaced a popular outdoor venue and, although the clients wanted to be able to ensure their shows would proceed regardless of the weather, whenever possible they also wanted to maintain the open-air atmosphere they were used to. The designers, therefore, created a building that could be constructed over a three-year phased programme that allowed the college to maintain its

Kalkin House

**Shelburne, Vermont, USA, 2001:
Adam Kalkin**

This building is located at the
Shelburne Museum where over
150,000 works of art are
exhibited in 39 separate buildings
in the museum grounds. Built in
2001, the Kalkin House is an
imaginative, contemporary
reinvention of a gallery contained
within a domestic space. An
industrial metal warehouse
building forms the external
skin with three ISO shipping
containers defining the interior
space. The building can be
completely opened up with
two double-storey glass garage
doors to completely change
its ambience.

normal summer schedule of performances and events. The principal transformable element is the roof, which is a hybrid pyramid composed of six identical triangular panels hinged along the bottom edge. The roof operates with a torque tube drive system that opens the panels simultaneously, creating a faceted emergence of the sky above the audience. A hydraulic safety mechanism ensures that the roof closes gently in the case of mechanical failure.

Buildings that change with the seasons articulate an important connection with the environment. A much more modest but nevertheless award-winning project is the architects Eightyseven's garden pavilion, built in Catalonia, Spain in 2004. A building of modest budget, it has two functions: a storage shed in the winter and an open-air room for the owner's adjacent house in the summer. Built from Ipê, a Brazilian hardwood from renewable resources, laminated glass and rusted steel, the building's walls slide and fold back to open it up completely to the immediate garden and distant views. With its unusual, segmented, geometric roof the building has the character of a sculpture and with its simple hand operation it has the quality and feel of a piece of furniture.

Transformations that enhance a building's connection with the external environment can also allow it to operate successfully in situations that would not normally be possible. For example, they can allow air and light onto a sports field

Garden Hut, Sant Miguel de Crilles, Spain, 2004: Eightyseven Architects.

so that the grass playing surface can grow, while allowing
protection from the weather when non-sporting events are
taking place. This is a comparatively passive way in which
the transformation enables a change of activity because the
shape of the space remains essentially unaltered. However,
moving walls, floors or roofs can also significantly change the
shape of a building so that different activities can take place.
A separate bedroom, study and lounge area can become a
large open-plan living space; a series of small meeting rooms
can become a single large conference area; a theatre can
extend its audience by adopting the foyer space.

In 1989, Jean Nouvel began work on the Lucerne
Cultural and Congress Centre in Switzerland, an arts project
for a prominent lake-front site that was principally created to
provide a contemporary home for the city's Festival of Music.
Chosen through competition and approved by a referendum
of the people of Lucerne, by its completion in 2000 the
design had developed into a complex, multi-purpose venue
containing a 1,900-seat auditorium, a flexible theatre for 900,
a conference centre and a museum of fine arts. A dramatic
feature of the building is its sweeping flat roof, under which
its diverse functions are sheltered. This projects 45 metres
(148 feet) out over a new terrace that borders the lake, and
has both aesthetic and practical functions. Aesthetically, it
reflects the lake and reprises its flatness in contrast to the

Kansas State University College of Architecture

Kansas, USA, 2004: KSU Live Project Studio

Vladimir Krstic was the architect for this extensive remodelling of the architecture school's early twentieth-century building, which was carried out in a collaborative design/build process by the students. New studios and review and meeting spaces were created in a dark windowless area, utilizing backlit walls to invest it with light. A more formal, tiered lecture theatre space is activated by a rotating wall that blocks access and light from an entranceway and provides a projection space.

mountains that surround the setting. Practically, it covers an external entry and event space that is intricately connected to the building's internal functions. In particular, the multi-purpose venue is designed to respond to this external space by having a stage that can reverse position and removable walls that enable the audience to be placed on opposite sides, bringing the external terrace into use.

Chuck Hoberman is a designer and inventor whose work explores transformable kinetic geometries that define space and structure, with deployable structures. He is best known for the Hoberman Sphere, a folding globe that expands into a larger form in a continuous action due to the geometric inter-linking of its components. Hoberman's designs are based on the concept of kinetic building blocks – linkages that connect to other linkages in order to transfer force, which is converted into motion. Assembling the kinetic building blocks into a complete network when they have the correct form and geometry creates a kinetic structure that can change shape or size with the application of force. The critical factor is for the kinetic structure to maintain stability, something that Hoberman defines as a process rather than a state. This can be achieved by restricting deflections in the structure's components.

Hoberman has built a number of building-scale structures, including the Hoberman Retractable Dome for the Expo 2000 in Hanover, Germany, and an Expanding Hypar

Hoberman Arch, Salt Lake City, USA, 2002: Chuck Hoberman.

Hoberman Arch, Salt Lake City, USA,
2002: Chuck Hoberman.

(short for hyperbolic parabaloid) for the California Science Center in Los Angeles, USA (1995). His largest project was for the Winter Olympic Games in Salt Lake City, USA in 2002. Here he created a 22 metre (72 foot) wide mechanical 'curtain' called the Hoberman Arch for the stage that hosted the opening and closing events of the Games, as well as the medal ceremonies each evening. Built by stage-set manufacturers Scenic Technologies, the curtain was a retractable semi-circular iris structure, 11 metres (36 feet) in radius, that when fully opened would stack into a compact 1.8 metre (5.9 foot) band. Constructed from sand-blasted structural aluminium and 96 translucent, fibre-reinforced panels, the curtain was operated by two 30 HP electric motors controlling tension cables that both opened it and supported its weight. More than 500 computer-controlled lights were integrated into the curtain's opening and closing action so that its appearance could be dramatically altered as it moved.

Movable elements that have the capacity to change a space's function also undeniably alter its character, both in the sense that it becomes physically different and also that it realizes its potential in a way that more conventional architecture cannot. Nevertheless, though the ambience of the space may change it is rare that this will alter the character of the entire building. This opportunity to affect the image or identity of architecture is a real possibility for

Floirac House

**Bordeaux, France, 1995:
Rem Koolhaas OMA**

The client of this house was
confined to a wheelchair,
so instead of providing a
conventional lift to access the
different levels, Koolhaas
created an elevating room that
forms a mobile core to the house.
This integrated the owner fully
into his domain and placed his
mobility at the centre of the
architectural statement.

Crate House

New York, USA, 1991:
Alan Wexler

Alan Wexler is a New York-based artist who originally trained as an architect. He creates sculptures and installations that reveal the importance of making objects in order to establish personal identity and our relationship to space and place. Crate House consists of a 'packed' dwelling that contains all the objects we are accustomed to having around us in a comfortable house. Seeing these in a form that can be transformed into an instantly anonymous, shippable object questions the true character of the modern home.

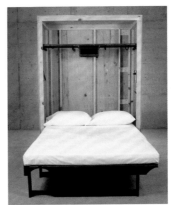

Kunsthaus, Graz

Austria, 2005: Peter Cook and Colin Fournier

A multi-purpose art centre, this building in the historic city centre of Graz contains exhibition, performance and multi-functional spaces within a translucent, curving acrylic-glass skin. A travelator draws people up from the transparent glazed ground floor, where there are meeting, shopping and catering spaces, into the exhibition spaces above. Beneath the curving skin on the building's east side is a low-resolution 'communicative display', designed by Realities United, called BIX (merging the words big and pixel). 295 circular fluorescent tubes can be individually controlled to create a greyscale display that can show simple messages and animations.

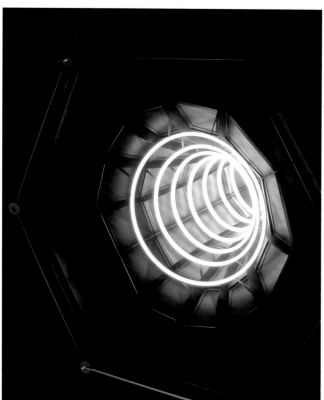

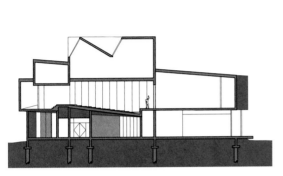

Art Department Building

Iowa University, USA, project 2005: Steven Holl

This extension to the Department of Art and Art History is intended to be an adaptable and responsive facility to accommodate the many different activities involved with art teaching and practice. The building is made from flat and curved oxidized steel plates that are folded and slotted together for strength. Flexible spaces open out from the studios in the summer and the horizontal passageways act as buffer zones with multiple roles.

**Milwaukee Art Museum, USA,
1994–2001: Santiago Calatrava.**

transformable design and it can be desirable for a range of reasons. For example, the building may need to establish different identities when it is open and when it is closed to the public, or it may need to change its image depending on the nature of the activity that is taking place inside.

The architecture of Santiago Calatrava regularly explores the potential of kinetic elements that have a particular affinity with his organic, expressive structures. His designs express the moment that occurs between balance and imbalance – a point in time and place where the structural design becomes most elegant. Many of his buildings consequently have elements that change shape or location, for example the glass-reinforced sculpture designed for the garden of the Museum of Modern Art, New York (1993) or the sliding, folding entrance doors to the underground station at Valencia's City of Arts and Sciences completed in 2000. Though designed with the functional purpose of a *brise soleil*, the sculptural element surmounting the entrance to Milwaukee Art Museum (2001) undoubtedly endows the roof of the building with a charismatic bird-like presence. The 72 steel fins of the structure weigh 90 tons and have a wingspan of 66 metres (217 feet), wider than a Boeing 747 aeroplane. Opening and closing the screen dramatically alters the light in the glass-covered entrance, which Calatrava describes as a welcoming gesture towards the visitors.

Calatrava's design for the replacement World
Trade Center Transportation Hub in New York City, due for
completion in 2009, also uses transformation for pragmatic
reasons, but it has an important symbolic agenda as well. The
new building not only replaces the New York underground
railway station that was destroyed in the disaster of 11
September 2001, but also links the New York subway with
commuter trains and ferry boats for this part of Lower
Manhattan. The main concourse for a building that will
eventually serve 80,000 passengers a day is an extremely
important part of the design and, because of the site's
history, its character had to both reflect the events that had
happened and also create something new and progressive.

The design is inspired by the great railway stations
of the nineteenth and early twentieth centuries, in particular
Penn Station, which it replaces, and mid-town's Grand Central.
It takes the form of an enormous glass roof that suffuses a
great space of movement and transition with natural light.
The two counterpoised canopies can be retracted
hydraulically to create a tapered opening, 15 metres (49 feet)
wide, to ventilate the building naturally and also to act as a
fire vent. Though the concourse has subtle memorial links
with the 2001 event – its main axis and the canopy's outer
edge align with the angle of the sun at the two critical
moments when the first tower was hit and the second

Galleria Mall West, Seoul, South Korea, 2004: UN Studio and Arup Lighting.

tower fell – Calatrava stresses that on the morning of 11 September each year the roof will open to act as a commemoration and to communicate an unprotected sense of connection with the sky.

Though physical transformation is the most potent form of change that a building can go through, it is important to note that highly significant visual transformation can also take place without physical movement. Possibilities for dramatic, instant alterations in the surface image of architecture have been accelerated by new mass communication devices, such as light-emitting diode (LED) screens. The Galleria Mall West in Seoul, South Korea was updated in 2004 by Dutch architects UN Studio, working with designer Rogier van der Heide of Arup Lighting. The building's exterior was wrapped in a new steel frame holding 4,340 glass discs, each of which includes an individually controlled LED panel. The entire façade has been turned into a giant programmable screen showing video, still images and text that can be controlled by the designer remotely via the Internet.

A much larger project using similar technology is Herzog and De Meuron's Allianz Arena in Munich, Germany (2005). It is a football arena for the two home teams, Bayern (who play in red) and TSV Munich (who play in blue). The building is clad in 2,816 rhomboid ETFE (Ethylene Tetrafluoroethylene Copolymer) cushions, suspended in an

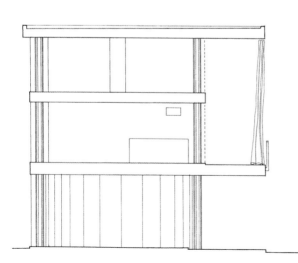

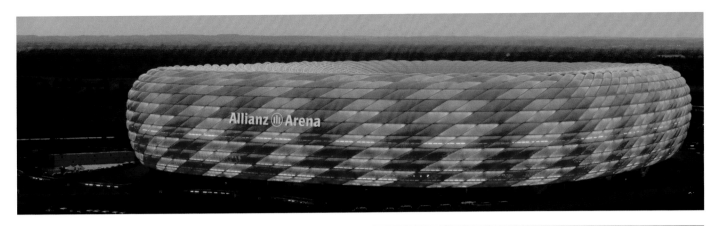

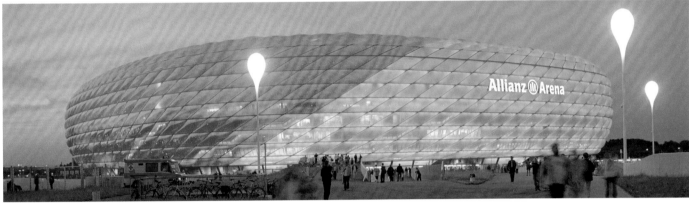

Allianz Arena, Munich, Germany,
2005: Herzog and De Meuron.

Curtain Wall House, Tokyo, Japan,
1995: Shigeru Ban.
Section and interior.

EPDM (Ethylene Propylene Diene Monomer) rubber clamping system that allows them to expand and flex. The LEDs are fixed around the edge of each cushion, which is printed with a pattern of white dots so that the light sources are diffused. The principal driver behind the concept was to turn the stadium blue or red, depending on which side was playing at home, but the flexibility of the LED system is such that the arena can be illuminated in a wide variety of messages and patterns, including pulsing and moving lights that make it appear to rotate.

As well as moving skins (walls and roofs) and surfaces (internal walls), transformation can also take place by moving entire elements. Japanese architect Shigeru Ban is known for his engagement with paper as a practical building material, but he does not just experiment with materials. Starting in 1991, he began a series of case-study houses that explored a range of different ideas associated with how architecture and design impact on the way people occupy their homes and the environment in which they are placed. Many of these houses explore the concept of disappearing boundaries – walls, roofs and partitions. Curtain Wall House was built on an urban site in Itabashi-Ku, Tokyo, Japan in 1995. The design reflects the openness of a traditional Japanese house, but instead of wood and paper *shoji* and *sudare* screens a large, two-storey tent-like curtain runs around the two open sides of the building's perimeter. This provides visual privacy, but still

SCI-Arc Boardroom and Event Space

Los Angeles, USA, 2003: Jones Partners

The Southern California Institute of Architecture occupies a historic former freight terminal in downtown Los Angeles. This meant the building structure could not be altered in any way to accommodate this project – a directors' boardroom, student café and event space. The problem was fitting three distinct functions into a space made for two and making an energetic intervention into this robust building. The result is a room that operates on a drawer principle, moving out through the side of the building. A large, industrial elevator adds further flexibility to the spaces, resulting in 24 separate arrangements in the way they can be configured.

House of Winds

Ibaraki, Japan, 2004: Takeyuki Okubo

Traditional houses in Japan have sliding screens, although these have to be removed in order to connect the rooms together to make one complete space. This contemporary reinterpretation is a house for two related families that has sliding walls, and windows that retract into the walls. This allows natural ventilation to pass through the entire house and also maintains views of the garden from deep within the building. The main circulation route takes a staggered path to allow privacy between the two families.

訂正・仕上構成図　2003.5.17

修正・2階仕上構成図　2003.5.17

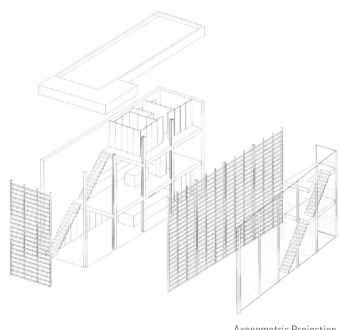

Axonometric Projection

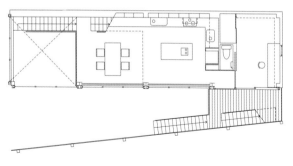

Second Floor Plan

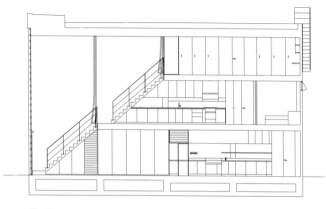

Section

allows ventilation and the noises of the street to penetrate the dwelling. In winter a set of glazed doors can be installed that combines with the curtain to improve insulation.

His Glass Shutter House (2004) revisits this idea on another Tokyo site in the Meguro district. This time it not only breaks down the boundary between inside and outside, but also between functions. The building can be described as a house with a restaurant on the ground floor or a restaurant with bedrooms above. In either case the Japanese sensibility for politely observed privacy is tested by the complete removal of the glass shutter walls. These can be retracted into the roof, though a curtain that is hung within the retracting façade can be deployed to obscure views in and out. Both functions are able to take advantage of the lofty, three-storey-high volume that faces onto the street.

Ban's Nine-Square Grid House (1997) in Hadano, Kanagawa Prefecture, Japan has a square plan that is divided into nine, smaller, square areas. The roof is supported along two sides by structural 'furniture', incorporating steel studs, that releases the other boundaries and the internal space from any further structural support. The open walls and the internal spaces can be divided by a series of floor-to-ceiling sliding panels that can be arranged in many different ways to accommodate functional needs depending on mood or season. These panels are neither walls, screens nor doors, but an extremely flexible system of enclosure that can reconfigure space in many different ways without affecting the area when removed.

In 2000, Ban designed a house in rural Kawagoe, Saitama, Japan that achieved a similar result, but in a far more straightforward manner. The brief from the client was that the family did not wish to be shut off within their own separate rooms, but wanted to live in a communal atmosphere with the possibility for privacy when necessary. The Naked House consists of a simple, rectangular, shed-like space made with a timber frame. The internal main space is bordered on one side by service rooms for storage, cooking and a bathroom, and on the other by a translucent and opaque wall. Internally, a group of mobile rooms can be moved about on wheels to any location, for example adjacent to a bathroom or a window. The rooms can be grouped together or stay separate and the family can sit inside, on top or outside of the rooms, or in the main space. The character of the home's space can be dramatically reconfigured in a moment by moving the rooms around to create barriers or openings.

Transformation can be found both in traditional architectural forms and in the most contemporary designs. It is of use for the smallest structures to the largest because transformation, though it can be difficult to achieve in a reliable and workable form, adds valuable efficiency to a

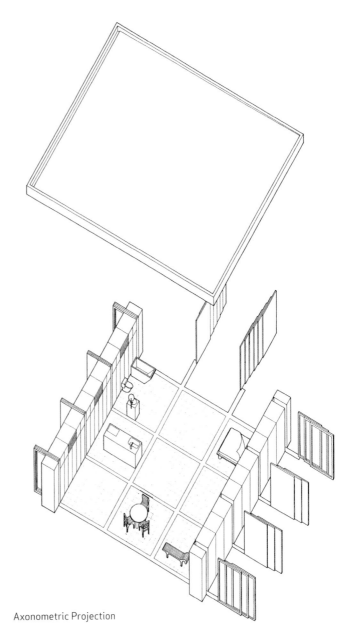

Axonometric Projection

Nine-Square Grid House, Hadano, Japan, 1997: Shigeru Ban.

NASA Bioplex Capsule

2000: Foreign Office Architects

This prototype project for the Future Homes exhibition explored how improved living accommodation could be provided for astronauts on NASA's planned 2013 mission to Mars. Because transportation would be in a confined, cylindrical spaceship, FOA designed a structure that would transform upon arrival into a stimulating building of great variety – a great benefit during the lengthy stays on the planet. A series of concentric ribs unfolds to change the extruded tube into a deformed cylinder that rotates along its length. Further ribs open up to create a larger space. The design challenges the restrictions placed on the form of the habitation module by the nature of its transportation. This strategy enables a form that extends and deforms from its original cylindrical unit to create unusual shapes and volumes.

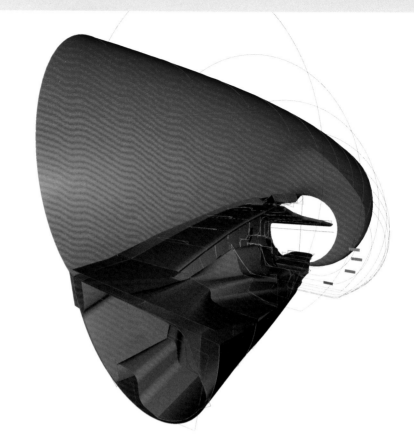

Office in a Bucket

London, UK, 2003: Inflate

This structure is an inflatable partition system made of polyurethane-coated, rip-stop nylon that arrives in a bucket no larger than an office wastebasket. Once plugged in and turned on it takes approximately eight minutes to inflate and creates a defined, private meeting space that can be stored in a very small space when not in use.

Naked House, Kawagoe, Saitama,
Japan, 2000: Shigeru Ban.

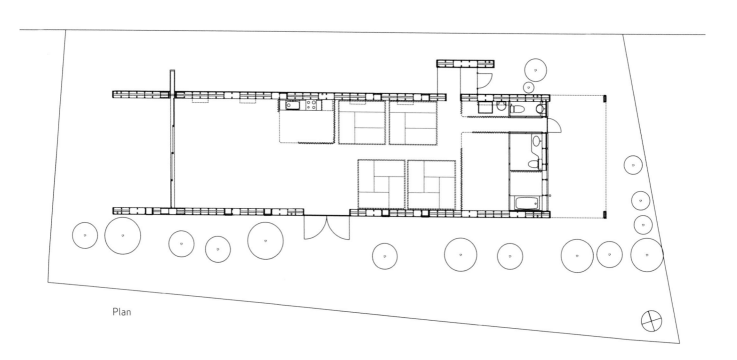

Plan

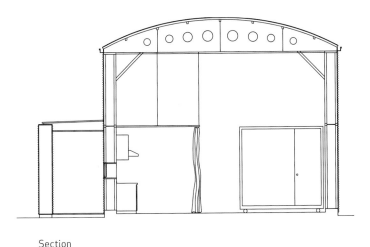

Section

building's functionality. It enables spaces to become more productive, to be used for different purposes or activities and by different groups at the same time. It also enables a unique connection with the external environment by opening up internal spaces to the outside. This guarantees the operation of events that are better undertaken in the open air, with a back-up enclosure system if the weather fails to co-operate.

Finally, it has the capacity to change human engagement with architecture in two important ways. Firstly, by creating an environment or an object that is not static it brings kinetic life to what is normally considered an inanimate art. Secondly, and perhaps most importantly of all, it creates a more democratic form of architecture. Though movable features are determined and incorporated into the design by the architect, their objective is to shift the building's finite form out of his or her control. It creates an indeterminate architecture, although within limits, that, as well as being more responsive, adds characteristics associated with events and performances that the user controls. Buildings that can significantly alter their shape over a limited time period establish a different sense of identity to wholly static ones, and people respond in a very different way to an environment that is motive than to one that is static. This is because their involvement with the building becomes an interaction rather than a simple reaction.

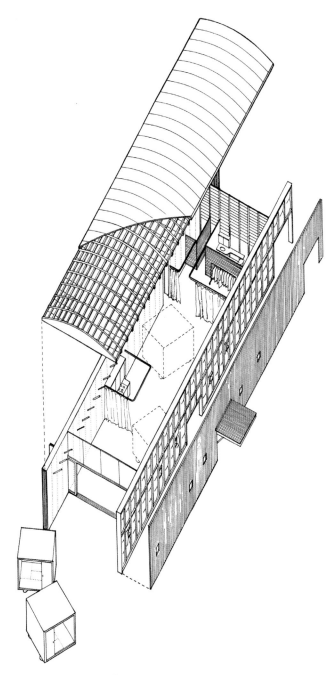

Axonometric Projection

Blue Moon
Groningen
Aparthotel

The Netherlands, 2001: Foreign Office Architects

This aparthotel is a four-storey building built on a cramped 5 x 5 metre (16.4 x 16.4 foot) site in the inner city that contains three short-let, open-plan flats. FOA's ambition was to create spaces that relate to the real nomadic environment of the tent. The interiors are clad in a silver fabric and the façade features a pattern of openings that allows occupants to reconfigure their environment from being totally closed to completely open.

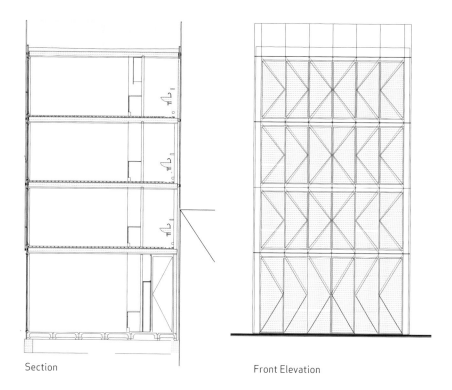

Section

Front Elevation

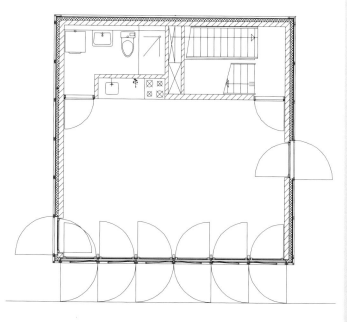

First Floor Plan

Brill House

Silverlake, California, USA, 1999: Jones Partners

Built on the foundation of a pre-existing building, this steel and glass structure is intended to develop a new technological vernacular. A three-storey open living space is on one side and the other contains private areas. Extensive display shelves for the owners' drum collection are accessed by a bicycle-operated travelling bridge – its guard rails can be deployed horizontally to provide a performance platform. A sliding screen system provides variable privacy and changes the acoustics of the building.

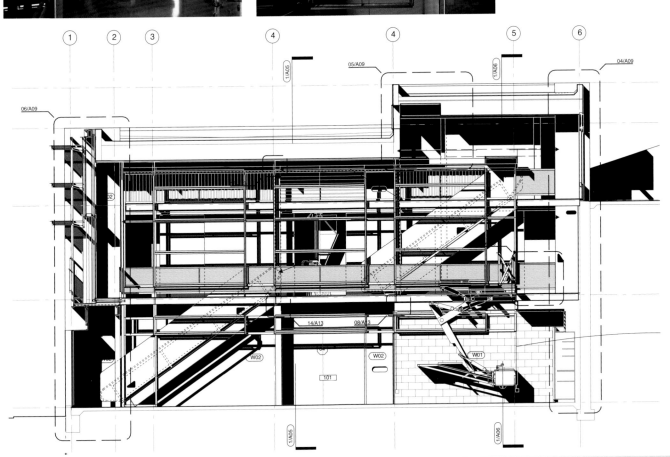

Move

Airtecture Air Hall, Germany, 1999: Festo KG.

The concept of a movable building appears at first to be an oxymoron. The very idea that the most substantial objects created by human beings can be designed to relocate from place to place seems almost to be a contradiction – buildings are the most permanent of our artefacts, but mobility is transitory. Deeper investigation, however, reveals that movable buildings are actually very common, and always have been. More surprisingly perhaps, the physical size and operational ambition for this type of architecture is consistently advancing. Movable architecture can be defined as buildings specifically designed to move from place to place so that they can fulfil their function better. In some cases mobility is absolutely necessary for them to fulfil their function at all. Although prefabricated buildings are becoming more common, they are not necessarily mobile. Most only use this method for the advantages in terms of quality and economy of construction, rather than the capacity for future relocation.

The most straightforward strategy for moving a building is to transport it in one piece. This 'portable' method has the clear advantage of the building being almost instantly available for use once it arrives at its new location. Some of these buildings have their transportation system incorporated into their structure, which can be regarded as a separate level of servicing that, like power, communications, water and drainage, is also dedicated to a specific aspect of its operation. The building may incorporate a specific structure, such as a chassis or hull, wheels, brakes and lights to aid with towing. The limitation for such buildings is size, particularly if they are to be relocated along the road network. Much larger structures are possible when floated; for example, there are many hotels that have been designed not primarily for transport, but to take advantage of city-based harbour-side settings.

It is sometimes remarkable that building functions that seem to be irreconcilable with mobility can be accommodated in movable facilities. The Screen Machine is the name given to a mobile cinema operation run by Highlands and Islands Arts Ltd (Hi-Arts). Based in Scotland to serve remote, rural communities, the organization's first cinema was built in 1999 – a specially constructed truck-based facility that was ultimately a compromise between a tight budget and the practicality of making a workable mobile auditorium. Consequently, its auditorium, which utilized

Screen Machine 2, UK, 2004:
Toutenkamion.

Screen Machine 2, UK, 2004: Toutenkamion.

pull-out volumes, took several hours to set up and needed constant and careful maintenance. Despite the limitations in its design, the cinema was in constant use and proved the concept to be a success. In 2001 it was deployed to Bosnia for four weeks to entertain the British troops who were serving there, and even provided the venue for a range of conferences and live performances. Subsequently, the facility has been used in more static situations where frequent relocation is not required.

When it came to replacing this valuable asset, Hi-Arts turned to the French coach-building company Toutenkamion to manufacture an improved version. This company has many years of experience in building specialist, hybrid building/vehicles including *Cinemobiles*. The new cinema takes the form of an articulated trailer that can be taken to any location that can be reached by road. It sits on hydraulic legs that provide a firm foundation when two sides of the truck are extended to make the raked auditorium. Access ramps and steps are set up separately. Screen Machine 2 has a set-up time of under an hour, more than 100 seats and is fully accessible to all. The cinema experience is of the same quality as it would be in a conventional building, with widescreen, surround sound and air-conditioning, which is an important factor in its success as audiences will no longer accept poor-quality presentations due to improved home video technology.

Strandbeest

The Netherlands, 2003–5: Theo Jansen

The Animaris Rhinoceros Transport is one of the 'Strandbeest' mobile sculptures by artist Theo Jansen. It has a steel skeleton with a polyester skin that appears to have a thick coating of sand from its beach location. Though it stands 4.7 metres (15.4 feet) tall and weighs two tons, the beast can be set in motion by just one person or on its own if there is sufficient wind. Rhinoceros Transport is one in a series of evolutionary *animaris* (the Latin name for beach animals) that Jansen has built. Rather than wheels they all use legs, which are much better for movement on soft surfaces, such as the beach.

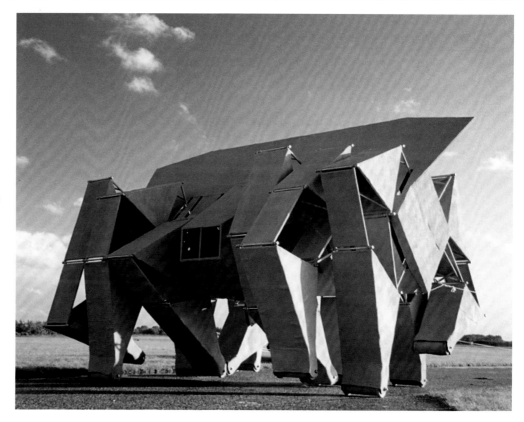

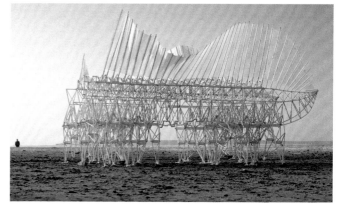

Mobile Dwelling Unit

USA, 2003: LOT-EK

The Mobile Dwelling Unit (MDU), by New York-based firm LOT-EK, is not just a single building, but also a concept that explores a completely different form of dwelling. Based on the standard ISO shipping container, the prototype MDU is a fully self-contained home that is transported in closed form using existing international infrastructures (trains, boats, trucks, cranes, etc.). When the MDU arrives at its location it is placed into a standard frame that provides infrastructure support. Service, seating, sleeping and storage compartments push out from the sides to free up the interior area for general living space.

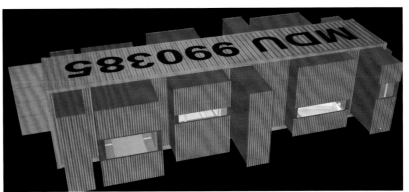

MV *Resolution*, Shanhaiguan
Shipyard, China, 2000.

MV *Resolution*, Shanhaiguan
Shipyard, China, 2000.

Based on the success of the Hi-Arts model, the Ministry of
Defence in the UK has now put its own mobile cinema into
operation travelling to sites where British troops are deployed.

Because it floats, the MV (master vessel) *Resolution*
can be a much larger facility than a wheeled structure. Part
boat, part factory and part hotel, this 14,574 ton, mobile, 135
metre (443 foot) long facility is specially designed to install
electricity-generating offshore wind turbines. Constructed by
the Shanhaiguan Shipyard in China, it is a hybrid structure
that has both a floating hull and foundations. The *Resolution*
travels to its work location under its own power. Once on site
it locates the turbine in position with a special frame by using
its main propulsion thrusters and three smaller bow
thrusters. It then jacks down its hydraulic legs, each of
which has 2,500 tons lifting capacity and 5,000 tons holding
capacity, to form a firm work base from which a hammer can
operate to drive the turbine's pile foundation into the seabed.
Once established on the seabed the *Resolution* can withstand
any type of weather with complete stability. On board, as
well as workshops associated with its principal role, there is
residential and leisure accommodation for the 35 crew and
up to 35 more construction operatives.

A more flexible approach to movable building design
is to create a facility that can be transported in a limited
number of dedicated parts, and then quickly assembled on

West McLaren Mercedes Team Communications Centre, UK, 2002: TAG McLaren.

site. This 'demountable' strategy allows many different architectural forms to be created, but more importantly it places no limit on the size of the finished building or its geographical location. Such buildings can be large and sophisticated and building functions include anything from a mobile administration centre to a concert hall. The downside of this method is that the building will not be in use as quickly as a portable type and its deployment process, as well as being slower, will also be more costly. Erection (and dismantling) may have to be carried out by trained personnel using special equipment, though this can be counter-balanced by the opportunity to include automatic erection equipment using hydraulics or other mechanical systems in the design. Wear and tear on the components that are regularly assembled and disassembled may also be greater. Special detailing to ensure weatherproofing is usually required at the junctions of the different building components.

Formula 1 Grand Prix motor racing is a glamorous peripatetic sport that revels in its high-tech image. Each season, teams of drivers, engineers and managers travel from circuit to circuit around the world accompanied by a circus of journalists, television crews and general hangers-on. The publicity side of Formula 1 is incredibly important because sponsors require maximum exposure of their team in order to justify the large sums of money they invest. For this reason,

Air Camper

UK, 2005: Inflate

Personal tents are incredibly popular leisure products and perhaps the most familiar type of mobile shelter. Despite improvements in materials for the membranes and the poltrusions (rods), design has not moved forward radically in the last 100 years. Inflate's concept for a pneumatic tent, however, is based around the prevalent use of the shelter in association with a vehicle. Using a car as a resource to produce the energy for inflation and for tethering changes not only the structural concept of the shelter, but also its image.

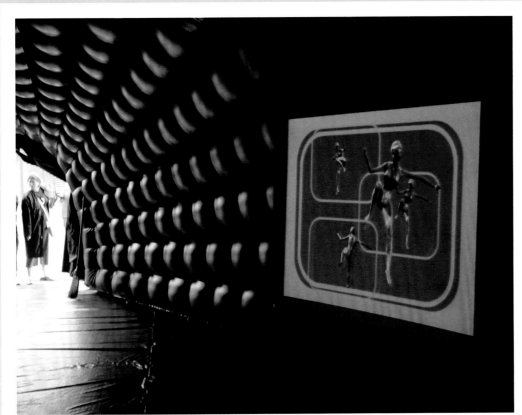

Big M

UK, 2005: Inflate

Bouncy castles are common, cheap, inflatable structures, and consequently their design is restricted by the need to make economic, price-conscious products. With Big M, Inflate has taken the same technology but pushed it further to create a more ambitious structure. Designed for a mobile exhibition of digital art, the building is transported in a single van together with the three people who erect and man it. Made from three identical panels that lace together to make a single environment, the compound form makes the space structurally stable. The exhibition is shown on flat screens in the darkened interior.

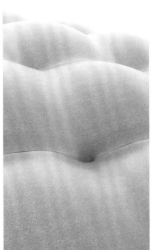

each circuit has a paddock where teams base their temporary homes for communications with sponsors and the media. These are specially designed, coach-built vehicles that accommodate the drivers' facilities, the engineers' work and meeting areas, team strategy offices and conference spaces and a media base for public-relations activities and visiting journalists.

TAG McLaren has always been at the forefront of developing sophisticated approaches to the problem of providing a working mobile building with an appropriate cutting edge, high-tech image. For the 2002 season they commissioned a completely new approach to this problem. Instead of using coach-based, hybrid vehicles they created a real building – the West McLaren Mercedes Team Communications Centre – that could be transported in 11 distinct components on six dedicated trucks that incorporate all the assembly equipment. The main strategy employed is a series of eight pods that are carefully positioned on the very restricted space that is allowed at each Grand Prix site. Each pod has its own hydraulic legs that lift it above the truck that it is transported on, which then backs out, before the pod lowers down to its final height. Subsequent pods are placed alongside and drawn horizontally into exact juxtaposition by hydraulic connectors. Two of the pods have upper stories that rise from the base also using hydraulics. The final component

West McLaren Mercedes Team Communications Centre, UK, 2002: TAG McLaren.
View over the paddock from the balcony; the atrium interior; and the rooftop air-conditioning plant.

Unipart Structure

UK, 2004: Inflate

This is UK design company Inflate's largest structure, 25 metres (82 feet) long and 8 metres (26 feet) high. It consists of two identical truncated cone shapes, laced together in the centre. Although externally it gives the impression of a completely inflatable building it is in fact a hybrid – a slender metal truss braced by cables supports the centre section. This makes it a far more economical structure to build, as an air beam of similar dimensions would need to be much higher performance and therefore a more costly construction element.

is a prefabricated, transparent pyramid roof that forms a covered atrium. Eight personnel can set up the entire building in just 12 hours. It includes a very sophisticated communications system, full electrics, air-conditioning, water supply and a drainage system – all of which can operate independently of external services.

The Halley British Antarctic research base does important work at a location where the hole in the ozone layer was discovered. It is located on the Brunt Ice Shelf where the ice is 150 metres (492 feet) thick, but the shelf is not static: it flows northward at a rate of 0.4 kilometres (0.2 miles) per year until it breaks off into icebergs. Consequently, a competition was launched in 2004 to find a replacement station, which will be in place for the 2008–9 season. The building must be able to withstand winter temperatures of -30°C (-22°F), have minimal impact on Antarctica's pristine environment and be mobile. Though this is a relatively stable platform there is real concern that cataclysmic change could take place causing a break-up in the ice beneath the new station, perhaps as early as 2010. The mobility of the building is important so that not only can it be built in its entirety away from the site, but also so that it can be relocated if (or when) ice conditions make this necessary. From 86 entries, six were short-listed and from these three winners were announced who were able to visit the site prior to developing their

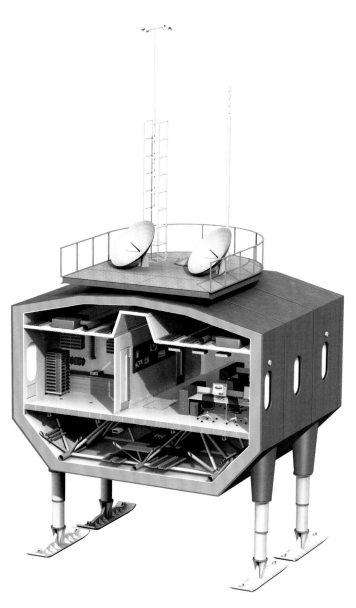

Halley VI Antarctica Base, project 2005: Hugh Broughton Architects/ FaberMaunsell Ltd.

**Halley VI Antarctica Base, project
2005: Hugh Broughton Architects/
FaberMaunsell Ltd.**

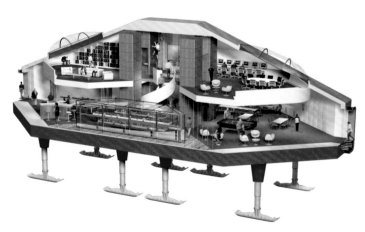

proposals. In September 2005 the final scheme for Halley VI was chosen – a design by FaberMaunsell Ltd (a firm of international engineers who have designed more Antarctic facilities than anyone else) in partnership with Hugh Broughton Architects.

Their design is based on a series of separate building modules, founded on skis to allow easy relocation and rearrangement of the facility if user requirements change, snow build-up becomes excessive or ice-shelf conditions alter. The largest module is centrally located and contains operations, communications, eating and recreation and a double-height hydroponics space. Other modules have work spaces, sleeping areas and power-generation facilities. The modules are light-weight, highly insulated sealed units that sit on legs helping reduce snow build-up. Interchangeable skis are fitted to allow the modules to be relocated by a tracked vehicle. A combined heat and power source will be used to support heating and airflow, low-energy lighting and domestic appliances – this is necessary because of the number of machines operated in the facility. Low water use is also important because of the energy required to make it from snow and also because of the low environmental impact concerns. A bio-digester will be used to create clean waste water and dry solids, which will be removed from Antarctica as part of the supply chain process.

Core module frames will be transported to Antarctica by ship, offloaded onto their skis and towed to the site by track-laying vehicles. Cladding panels and skeletal frames for the large module will all be fixed mechanically to ensure easy dismantling when the building is eventually decommissioned. Once the shell is complete, the fit-out can continue over the winter period within protected enclosures. The designers have integrated the most extreme building performance criteria required anywhere on the planet into a mobile building strategy that can also provide a real sense of comfort and identity for workers spending large periods of time isolated more than 16,000 kilometres (10,000 miles) away from the UK.

The most flexible form of movable building is one that is built using a componentized system that may be assembled in different ways. This 'modular' system has numerous advantages. The building may be capable of assembly in varied forms and layouts, making it suitable for alternative functions and different types and sizes of sites. Because there are more components, the building breaks down into smaller and more compact parts, consequently making transportation easier and more efficient. Using standardized components means that assembly is less dependent on the kit-of-parts concept, where every part must have a corresponding connecting part. Also, delays can be avoided because standardized spares can be carried if damage

Desert camp for the UN: Weatherhaven Resources Ltd, Burnaby, Canada.

Mobile shelter in Franz Josef Land, Arctic Ocean, Russia: Weatherhaven Resources Ltd, Burnaby, Canada.

occurs. However, there are also problems with this system. Because of the large number of parts, assembly and disassembly can be very complex, requiring a much greater number of junctions and joints. A larger erection team and greater erection period will probably be required with detailed plans and instructions, which can result in a greater capacity for things to go wrong. There are also fewer opportunities for building in labour- and time-saving automatic assembly systems because construction components are relatively small and numerous.

Weatherhaven Resources Ltd, based in Burnaby, British Columbia, Canada, provides flexible building resources that can be located anywhere in the world at short notice. Typically, their portable, demountable, modular, mobile buildings are used in remote, sometimes extreme, locations for research, prospecting or industrial operations such as mining. Their facilities are created using componentized building systems that are simple yet sophisticated, allowing customized solutions built around a series of basic building types. The portable Mobile Work Camp can be towed behind vehicles on wheels or skis, enabling shelter support to be relocated on a daily, or even hourly, basis. The demountable Mobile Expandable Container Camp is based on an ISO shipping container that can be transported on standard vehicles. When it is positioned on site, the sides let down

Arctic camp: Weatherhaven Resources Ltd, Burnaby, Canada.

Shelter assembly: Weatherhaven Resources Ltd, Burnaby, Canada.

Mobile Classroom

Richmond-on-Thames, London, UK, 2005: Future Systems

The 2002 British Government Classrooms of the Future initiative sought to create a new kind of mobile school building that would bring together factory-based manufacturing and the latest ideas in teaching environments. These pods are innovative replacements for the conventional mobile classrooms that dominate the playgrounds of expanding and contracting schools. Nicknamed 'tic-tacs' by the children, after an elliptically shaped candy of the same name, the building's structural skin is made of fibreglass and balsa wood. The building functions independently with its own heating and toilet, though the latter has to be connected into the mains drainage system.

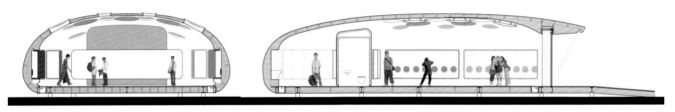

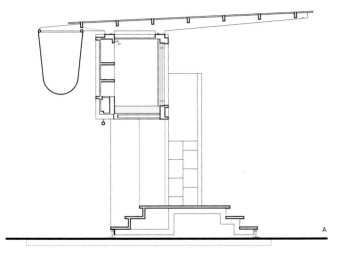

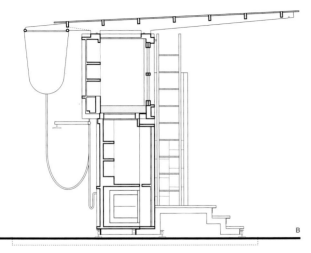

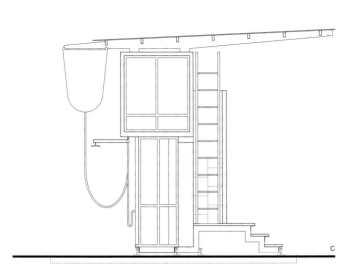

La Petite Maison du Weekend

Columbus, Ohio, USA, 1998: Patkau Architects

This project was designed as an exploration of the minimal, sustainable, self-sufficient dwelling and was constructed for the Fabrications Exhibition at the Wexner Center for the Arts in Columbus, Ohio. The building can be towed to any vehicle-accessible site, where it is opened out into its deployed form. Made from solid and ply hemlock wood with steel strengtheners at critical joints, it consists of a shelter, sleeping loft, kitchen, composting toilet and shower. Water is collected from the roof and photovoltaics are used to generate electricity for lighting, a high-efficiency refrigerator and a small fan in the toilet.

and a membrane tent covering triples the floor area. Fixed equipment, built into the centre of the container, is immediately ready for use.

The primary Weatherhaven structure, however, is a modular system based on a tented, arched-frame building, to which can be added insulated floors, suspended ceilings, internal partitioning and various levels of environmental equipment, including full air-conditioning. All the buildings are designed to be fitted into standard shipping crates for truck, ship or air transportation. Clients can arrange for the facility to be erected by trained personnel, so that they just walk into a fully operating set-up, or they can have the entire building packaged up with a set of instructions for assembly by their own operatives when they arrive. The systems include full servicing equipment for power, water supply and drainage, and are capable of operating on a no-impact basis in sensitive environments where everything that is shipped in has to be shipped out, including all waste products. The components are designed to be no heavier or larger than a human being can handle, so no heavy machinery needs to be resourced. They are also capable of being used in different scenarios for maximum efficiency, so the same basic shelter can be used in both hot and cold climates providing that the correct additional insulation, ventilation and heating components are incorporated.

Nomadic Museum, New York, USA, 2005: Shigeru Ban.

Axonometric Projection

Move

A completely different way of creating modular mobile buildings is to combine a dedicated design that has a limited number of special parts with standard components that are available at multiple locations. Tadao Ando achieved this with his design for the Karaza Theatre in 1987, a building made primarily from standard scaffolding components with the addition of the theatre group's red tent roof, their props and scenery. In 2005, Shigeru Ban realized a wholly new building concept for a travelling art show by international photographic artist Gregory Colbert. After selling out his *Ashes and Snow* show at the Venice Biennale in 2002 it was suggested to Colbert that he remount the exhibition, in its entirety, in other cities. The first location for Ban's building was on a Manhattan pier on the Hudson River, New York, USA. The Nomadic Museum utilized a standard, universal component – the shipping container. 148 ISO containers were stacked in a self-supporting grid, assembled by a floating crane, to form a substantial temporary building – wire-braced fabric, infill walls and roof complete the building envelope. Internally, a wooden plank runway, flanked by river stones, defines the visitor's route and Colbert's photographs are suspended between paper-tube columns that help support the roof. When the exhibition moves (other destinations include Beijing and Paris) the components are shipped in 14 of the ISO containers with the remaining 134 containers being sourced close to the site.

Nomadic Museum, New York, USA, 2005: Shigeru Ban.

Section

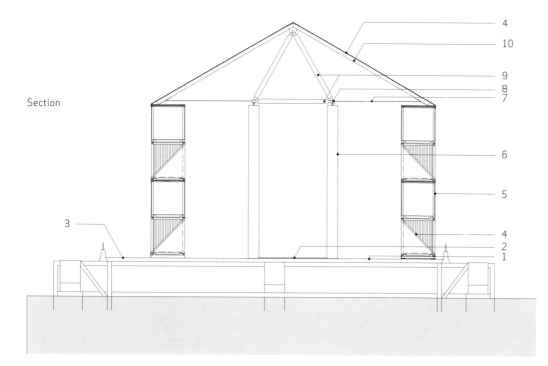

Nomadic Museum, New York, USA, 2005: Shigeru Ban.
1. Gravel
2. Wooden runway
3. Existing pier
4. PVC roof membrane
5. Shipping container
6. 76cm (30in) diameter paper-tube column, 2.5cm (1in) wall thickness
7. Horizontal brace: steel cable
8. Steel channel strut, 28 x 19cm (11 x 7.5in)
9. 30.5cm (12in) diameter paper-tube truss, 2.5cm (1in) wall thickness
10. Steel rafter 17.8 x 25.4cm (7 x 10in)

UK '98
Festival
Pavilion

Japan, 1998: Klein Dytham

Virgin Airways was one of the sponsors of this mobile pavilion that promoted a year-long series of British-themed cultural events in Japan. The structure consisted of five separate elements that could be assembled in a number of different patterns. The cloud-like roof (with a Virgin aeroplane tail protruding) was supported on an aluminium framework to which translucent walls could be attached when privacy or weather protection was required. Seating boxes at the base provided the foundations of the structure.

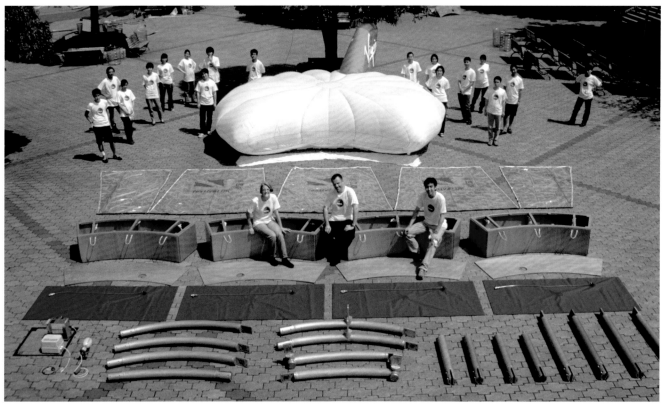

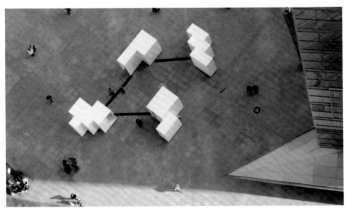
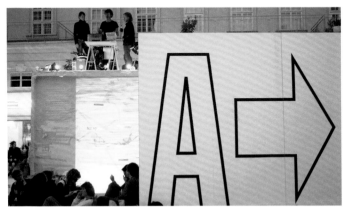

Mobile Museums, Germany, 2004:
Public Art Lab/Gruber + Popp
Architekten.

Each of these three movable building strategies – portable, demountable and modular – can be used with a wide range of construction forms. One form of construction is volumetric. This consists of pre-assembled, factory-built 'spaces' that are transported as complete buildings or as parts of buildings. This type of product began life as a site hut, but can now fulfil many functions. When created as 'wall-less' structures, volumetric buildings can be assembled into much larger buildings. They can also be manufactured with built-in services and interior and exterior finishes, thus increasing the speed of deployment and reducing construction time. However, transportation is expensive with large, empty internal volumes reducing efficiency. Another form of construction is flat-pack. Flat-pack buildings need rigid surfaces, but reduce transportation inefficiencies by collapsing into layered panels when being relocated. External and internal surface finishes can be applied in the factory and more complex shapes can be created in the finished product because a range of different forms can be designed into the assembly system. Greater on-site erection time is, however, a necessity and junction detailing is more critical as this is no longer factory-controlled.

Berlin-based arts agency Public Art Lab, with architects Gruber + Popp, created the Mobile Museums project in 2004. It was based around the concept that relatively modest 'buildings', such as phone boxes, could

**Carlos Moseley Music Pavilion,
New York, USA, 1991: FTL Design
Engineering Studio.**

change the nature of public spaces. They created a group of cube-like, volumetric structures that can be transported on trucks and off-loaded and relocated with a standard forklift truck. The buildings are temporarily located in densely occupied urban locations, such as city squares, and form the focus for collaborating artists who take over the buildings and the intervening spaces for sculpture, events and performance.

Tents are perhaps the most familiar and archetypal mobile buildings, and recent material innovations have dramatically expanded their potential. Advanced tensile fabrics that are flexible, strong and environmentally stable have enabled more advanced computer-aided design methods that have resulted in efficient structures that can enclose large spaces with low building mass. Twin-layer membranes can also make these structures more environmentally efficient, and a wide range of opacity and surface treatments can create different character interiors. There is already a wide range of commercially available, tensile-membrane mobile buildings and this form of construction is still being explored for dedicated building designs that push its capabilities even further. Tension structures use struts and cables for support and bracing, creating evocative and elegant shapes.

FTL Design Engineering Studio has created a number of tension structure buildings that fulfil a wide range of

Structural Plan

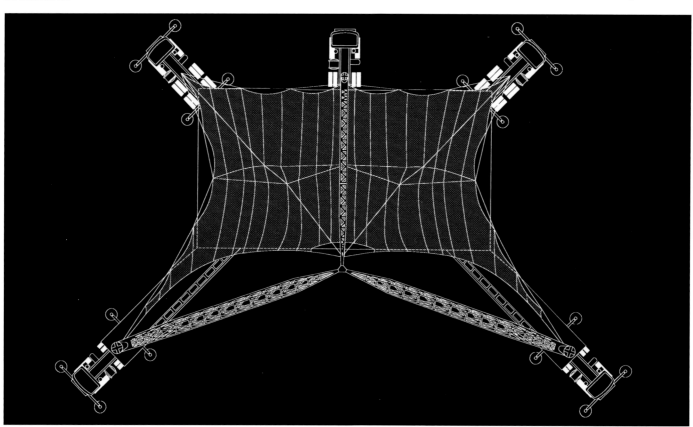

Harley-Davidson Machine Tent, USA, 2002: FTL Design Engineering Studio.

Assembly Procedure

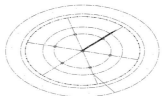
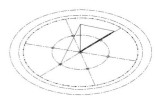

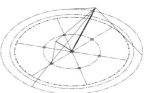
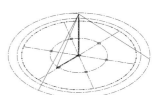

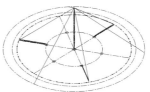
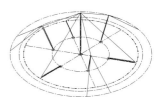

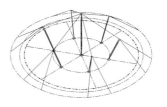

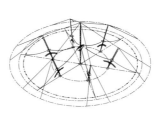

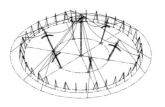
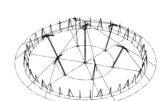

functions, from retail development and convention halls to performance buildings. One of their most important structures is the Carlos Moseley Music Pavilion, which, although it was first commissioned in 1991, is still in regular use each year for a series of outdoor classical music performances in the New York parks. The concept was to create a structure that could provide facilities to make concert hall-quality performances available externally and to a large audience. The facility consists of a 21 metre (69 foot) high tripod structure that is built onto five standard flatbed trucks. This supports a PVDF (Polyvinylidene Difluoride) Teflon-coated, polyester fabric membrane that provides a dramatic backdrop for the performance, particularly when lit at night. More importantly it also provides a semi-rigid rain cover and sound reflector to project acoustically the music towards the audience. Concert-hall acoustics are replicated by a sophisticated Bose sound system that can build in reverberation time that would normally only be heard indoors.

FTL's Machine Tent for the Harley-Davidson Travelling Tour 2002–3 was an exhibition building that was created to commemorate the motorcycle manufacturer's 100th anniversary. Externally, it is reminiscent of a conventional, single-pole tent, but it actually has a total of seven masts – a central primary one and six secondary ones that form a

Eco Lab

Los Angeles, USA, 1998: Office for Mobile Design

Architect Jennifer Siegal designed this mobile classroom for a non-profit-making organization, The Hollywood Beautification Team, to communicate environmental and sustainability issues to children in Los Angeles schools. Built with donated and recycled building materials and a truck trailer base by students from Woodbury University, the standard vehicle has been transformed into a mobile example of how cheap and adapted materials can still make interesting and flexible architecture.

Portable Construction Training Center

Los Angeles, USA, 1999: Office for Mobile Design

The PCTC is a mobile teaching workshop to enable courses in plumbing, painting, carpentry, plastering and electrical installation to take place on site where the actual building construction is taking place. Built for the non-profit-making organization Venice Community Housing Corporation, it is made entirely from donated and recycled building materials by students of Woodbury University. The building opens out when it arrives at its site to form a series of porches, each of which is dedicated to a different skill and contains the appropriate tools and facilities.

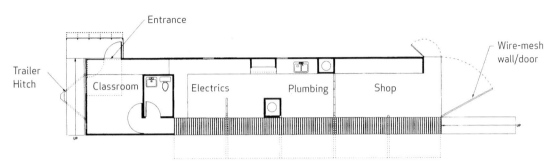

Entrance

Trailer Hitch

Wire-mesh wall/door

Classroom

Electrics

Plumbing

Shop

Floor Plan

Valhalla

Sheffield, UK, 1999: Rudi Enos

The largest tented structure in the world is the Valhalla system designed by Rudi Enos and operated by Gearhouse Structures in the UK. It is a modular building that can be erected in several different formats depending on requirements, but at its largest it can cover a ground area of 20,352 square metres (219,200 square feet) or 2.04 hectares (5.03 acres). The building uses up to 20 masts, each 24 metres (79 feet) high, which as well as supporting the tent can also support almost limitless amounts of scenery, lights and special effects. This building requires no external cranes for erection as it has its own built-in power winches to raise the membrane, which can be either translucent or blackout depending on the event requirements.

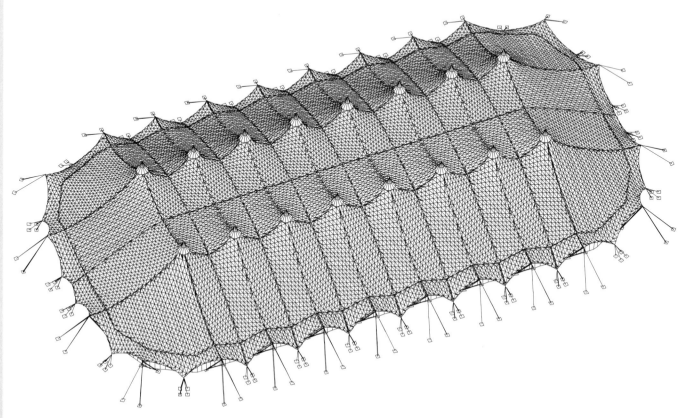

hexagon on plan. Though the structure is 50 metres (164 feet) in diameter, it can be erected without extra equipment, using only the winches that are wired within the masts to haul up the elevated components. The masts are also used to carry lighting and communication equipment associated with the exhibition. An important feature of the building was that it had to meet the safety and construction codes of all the countries it was visiting (including Australia, Canada, Mexico and Japan). This is an issue that often adds to the complexity of designing mobile buildings that will travel to international destinations.

There is another form of tensile membrane design that also creates dramatic visual results – pneumatic architecture. Air-supported buildings utilize varying air pressure to support enclosing structures, sometimes in combination with cables for bracing but usually without any other compressive struts. There are two types of air-supported structures: low pressure and high pressure. Low-pressure buildings work by enclosing a slightly higher internal air pressure, not noticeable to occupants, that ensures the building skin maintains its form – entry and exit from low-pressure buildings must be done through an air lock. Low-pressure air-supported architecture can take a wide range of forms, but most have large spans, as this is a prime benefit of this choice of structure. Large mobile buildings of this type can be difficult to achieve because it involves moving vast expanses

Airquarium, Germany, 2001: Festo KG.

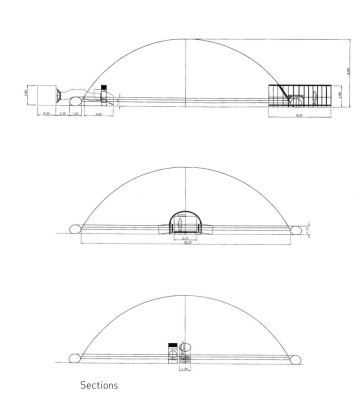

Sections

of continuous membrane about on site, but also because of the problems encountered with maintaining large airtight joints for the structure to work.

High-pressure buildings use the principle of air-beams that become rigid when inflated. The problem, until recently, with air-beams has been that the air pressures for anything other than small buildings are so extreme that joints have not been reliable. Recent improvements in materials, design and manufacture are, however, resulting in practical buildings of substantial size. These structures have significant advantages over low-pressure alternatives. The buildings can be transported in smaller components, the building skin can be separated from its structure, large lengths of airtight joints are not required, and air locks at the entrances are not necessary. All this makes erection and deployment much faster; however, there is the danger of fast 'cataclysmic' collapse if a number of beams are punctured simultaneously.

Festo KG are an international company specializing in making pneumatic operating systems that power manufacturing industry robotics. Their Corporate Design section is a dedicated 'blue-sky' research facility that finds new uses for the technology the company has developed. This includes architecture and building designs that utilize both low- and high-pressure pneumatic membranes. The Airquarium (2001) is a 32 metre (105 foot) diameter, air-supported dome that

Airquarium, Germany, 2001: Festo KG.

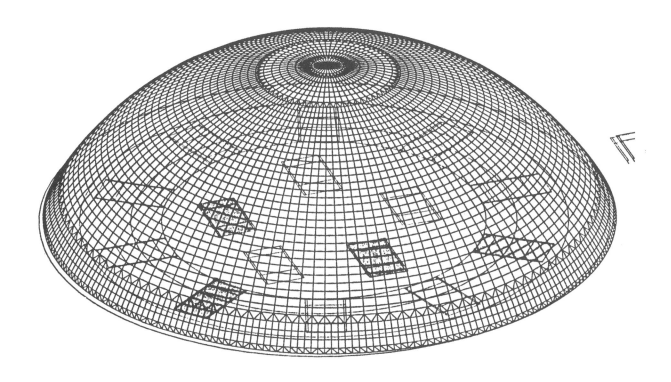

Airtecture Air Hall, Germany, 1999:
Festo KG.

is used as a single volume transportable exhibition and event space. Its Vitroflex membrane is remarkable for its high level of translucency and also for the safety factors built into its chemical make-up – if it catches fire only a non-toxic vapour of water and vinegar is released. The building is restrained around its perimeter by a water-filled torus (hence the name Air-*quarium*) and is transported in two small standard containers, one of which contains the dome and the other the supporting pump equipment.

The Airtecture hall (1999) is a mobile, rectangular meeting and exhibition space that utilizes a number of innovative high-pressure structural systems. It consists of three main elements: air-filled 'Y'-shaped columns, tensioned by cables and a series of linear pneumatic muscles; air-filled flat panel walls; and air-filled roof beams. The 'Y'-shaped columns are like twenty-first-century flying buttresses and give the building a remarkably original quality. The pneumatic muscles that help tension the building are active structural members that can be automatically loosened or tightened depending on external wind pressures. The air-filled flat panels are 20 centimetre (7.9 inch) thick 'mattresses' that incorporate cross threads spanning between two membranes to provide stiffness under 0.5 bar (7.3 pounds per square inch) pressure. There are also window areas that consist of transparent air pillows between the opaque walls. The 12.7

The Retreat

UK, 2004: Buckley Gray Yeoman

Mobile holiday homes are ubiquitous 'temporary' buildings, scattered throughout the countryside of Europe and North America – they are a popular yet often unattractive form of development. The Retreat is one of a number of designs that seeks to redress this situation by treating the caravan as real mobile architecture, creating contemporary spaces made with quality materials and built on sustainability and low-energy principles.

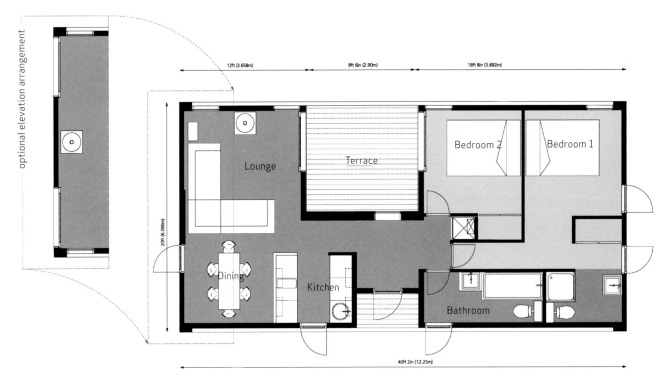

optional elevation arrangement

12ft (3.658m)   9ft 6in (2.90m)   18ft 8in (5.692m)

20ft (6.096m)

Lounge

Terrace

Bedroom 2

Bedroom 1

Dining

Kitchen

Bathroom

40ft 2in (12.25m)

Floor Plan

Mobile Studio

Pompidou Centre, Paris, France, 2004: Shigeru Ban Architects

Because it would be uneconomic to rent a studio in Paris for the three-year duration of the Pompidou Metz design process, Shigeru Ban Architects have designed a temporary paper building on the sixth-floor terrace of the famous Piano and Rogers designed building. Prototyped by students at Keio University in Japan and built by local architecture students in Paris, the building is designed to be relocated when it reverts to the ownership of the client at the end of the three-year period of SBA use.

Airtecture Air Hall, Germany, 1999: Festo KG.

metre (41.7 foot) long roof beams vary in diameter from 75 centimetres (30 inches) at the ends to 125 centimetres (50 inches) in the centre. Though designed to be mobile, the original building was in such demand at the company's headquarters in Esslingen, Germany that a second version had to be made as an exhibition piece for Festo products on tour.

Though modular, volumetric, flat-pack, tensile and pneumatic are the primary building construction options, many buildings do not use just one system exclusively but instead combine them to make use of their various advantages to solve particular problems. For example, tension structure buildings can use flat-pack panels to form a perimeter wall for security or privacy reasons. An air-supported building may utilize a volumetric structure not only to house support services such as the pump used to inflate it, but also as a container for protection during transportation.

Movable architecture often crosses over with other fields of design and consequently has frequently made use of cultural and technological transfer. Traditional forms of movable building are the roots of all architectural design – the tent and the *yurt* are quintessential built forms that are the mobile precedents for the pyramid and the dome. The most common mobile buildings are produced by industry – the mobile volumetric buildings produced by UK-based manufacturers Portakabin and Terrapin, among many others.

Caravans and trailers are both vehicles and buildings – the Airstream in particular has been an influence on both architects and product designers as an iconic example that epitomizes freedom. Product designers are often commissioned for this sort of work because they are rightly perceived as pursuing an empirical approach to solving the problem at its root. Consequently, mobile architecture makes use of strategies and techniques that are found in a range of industries – architecture, transportation, structural, mechanical and services engineering and the design of the operational object. Vehicle designers and transportation engineers are also used to creating bespoke mobile environments based on a range of stock components.

But the movable building is architecture. It has the same primary function as static architecture, which is to meet the users' requirements in a wide range of practical and aspirational ways. It also has the same impact on people that permanent architecture has in that it helps to identify a sense of place and to create lasting memories. Although the place may not necessarily be a specific geographic location, and the architecture may alter its site after a limited time, it still has a lasting and meaningful impact. Human experience is filled with memories that stem from a fleeting event yet leave a permanent presence. Movable architecture expands our experience of a place dramatically, helping us to realize

our needs and aspirations in an immediate and practical manner, and also to add understanding to what a place means by seeing it change. Movable architecture can fulfil all the functions of permanent architecture and can vary in size from the smallest portable shelter to a giant 10,000-seat auditorium. It can also be there one day and gone the next, allowing it to make use of environmentally or historically sensitive sites and to give people a taste of innovative architecture in a way that would not be possible for a permanent building.

Interact

R128 House, Stuttgart, Germany, 1999–2000: Werner Sobek.

The success of humanity as a species is dependent on our ability to act and react – to recognize and analyse situations and respond to them in an appropriate manner. We do not always get it right, but history has shown that we do the right thing often enough, as the general trend is towards improvement of our circumstances. As technology has improved and had a greater impact on our lives, more and more energy has been devoted to the development of automatic systems that make things happen faster and with greater efficiency. Automation can take two forms: an action that is carried out to a predetermined, unchangeable pattern; and an action that is carried out towards a predetermined result though the process may be changed along the way. The second form can be described as intelligent automation, the key difference being that it has a built-in, reactive quality. In architecture, the inclusion of some form of intelligent building system is becoming more and more common. However, the industry is not a leader in this field but a follower of others, such as the automotive industry.

The ambition of intelligent building is to integrate sensor systems that assess the internal and external environment and the condition of the building's systems and then act on this to achieve maximum operational performance and comfort levels. In this way the building, in effect, cooperates with its inhabitants to achieve the best conditions possible. The areas in which intelligent building systems operate are environmental comfort, safety, security, privacy, sanitation, communications, entertainment, ambience, energy-use and efficiency. These systems and requirements, though of value in the individual building, must also be linked to external systems, such as global telecommunications, the Internet, external services and entry and physical access arrangements.

Intelligent automation requires two main components: something that identifies what is happening – a sensor; and something that carries out an appropriate action in response – an actuator. This is the simplest form of system, but there may be many more components in a complex arrangement, perhaps the most common being a computer to provide an interface and to maintain overall control. The pressure for increased intelligence in buildings comes from perceived improvements that will lead to performance increases and greater safety. The way that this is achieved is by creating systems that have greater accuracy, reliability and lower maintenance. The trend is towards developing sensors that

are smarter, more adaptable and are grouped so they become self-calibrating and self-diagnosing, with fault recovery protocols in the case of failure. Miniaturization, standardization and integrating sensors with actuators will lead to lower costs, higher volume production and more widespread use. These intelligent building systems are already well on their way to becoming standard consumer products with mass-market magazine and media coverage of their development and implementation.

Intelligent building systems are used to create interactive architecture that responds to users' requirements in automatic or intuitive ways. It is architecture that is receptive to people's needs to alter their environment and has mechanisms in place to do this easily. Interactive architecture changes appearance, climate or form by sensing the need for change and responding to it automatically. It uses sensors that can receive signals directly from individuals or groups, from the devices they habitually use, such as mobile phones, PDAs or computers, or the effects they automatically have on the environment, such as air movement or temperature change. These sensors operate actuators that can trigger a wide range of actions – kinetic systems that physically alter space, services that alter the environment or materials that alter their state. Interactive architecture enables people to engage with architecture, not

TV Tank

New York, USA, 1998: LOT-EK

LOT-EK is the New York-based architects and artists Giuseppe Lignano and Ada Toller. Their work crosses the boundary between architecture and art with installations and speculative design being as much a part of their work as architecture and interiors. They often use robust, used industrial products as a basis for reinvention – in this case an old petroleum trailer tank was cut into sections to form a series of cells where individuals can lounge and watch television. This contemporary art/architecture, installation/facility was relocated to John F. Kennedy Airport, New York in 2004.

Mixer

New York, USA, 2000: LOT-EK

This project was constructed for an installation at the Henry Urbach Architecture Gallery in New York. It consists of the bowl from a concrete mixer adapted to form a cocoon that remains connected to the outside world through audio-visual equipment. The robust, industrial form creates the ultimate protective shell, allowing inhabitants to be completely secluded while still connected through the electronic media they control.

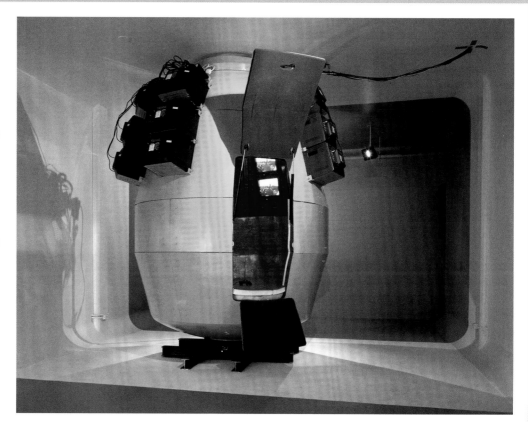

as passive creatures existing in a static set of conditions, but as proactive individuals affecting the space that they inhabit.

The most common form of interactive architecture is one that changes its climatic environment automatically to respond to changes brought about by external weather conditions or internal activity by occupants or machines. Internal sensors monitor temperature, humidity and in some cases carbon dioxide levels. External sensors monitor weather conditions, including direct sun and overcast conditions. Typically, these then automatically actuate heating and air-conditioning systems that work on room or zone controls, pre-set by the user to their own preferences. Other common environmental controls relate to energy efficiency – sensors that switch off lights when people leave rooms, turn off the water supply, close external doors or shut down escalators when they are not required. Future developments in environmental control will begin to use predictive technology to improve efficiency and accuracy. For example, domestic systems may be able to sense when inhabitants are about to return home via their mobile phone signals or vehicle links and so prepare the house environment for their arrival. Also, sensors that link to an individual's physical condition may be able to tune environmental settings so that comfortable temperatures and humidity are maintained. Intelligent systems for safety and security are also common features of contemporary buildings – operating alarms, links to emergency services and specialist equipment in case of fire, natural disaster or intruders. These might also be extended to monitor the health of inhabitants for home diagnosis and care.

With the desire to further reduce energy costs, it is now becoming common for sophisticated sensors to operate mechanical systems in partnership with traditional, passive means of energy control – for example, opening vents, windows or roofs for ventilation, or sun blinds and a *brise soleil* for shading. This strategy is delivering a form of interactive architecture that changes the actual form of the building, depending on users' requirements. Façades that react to sunlight like the iris of a human eye or the petals of a flower or become opaque when the need for privacy is detected are useful not only to the building inhabitants, but also act as a signal to those outside the building that something is going on, that activity is taking place and that the architecture is active.

The area where development is happening most rapidly is in the appearance of buildings. Instead of a static form, designed as a definitive assembly of permanent materials at the building's inception, some architects are now exploring façades that are programmed for change. Since cinematic moving pictures were developed, it has been possible for

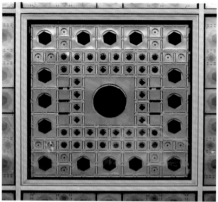

Arab World Institute, Paris, France,
1989: Jean Nouvel.

architecture to be altered by over-layering images projected
onto the building in the hours of darkness. This technique was
enhanced when lasers were developed so that images could
also be seen in daylight, although the nature of laser
projection is limited to a relatively small number of graphic
forms. The introduction of large-format television screens,
and more recently LED systems, has made it possible for
buildings to have continuously changing visual images on
their façades. It is important to note, however, that if the
display on the building's façade does not have an interactive
element that responds to those who see it, then these new
technologies will be doing little more than continuing the
pre-determined architectural forms of the past. Though it
may cause a reaction in the viewer, external remote control
of images on a façade is still not truly interactive.

The form that interactive design takes depends, to
a great extent, on the technological system employed in its
realization. Essentially there are three principal methods that
can be employed: mechanical systems; assembled non-moving
systems; and solid-state materials. All of these must be
triggered by some system of sensors and actuators and the
more complex ones may require separate control devices,
usually computer based. Paradoxically for a strategy that
leads to flexibility, these methods become more advanced in
design with the less movement that actually takes place. This

Transports

**The Netherlands, 2000:
Kas Oosterhuis**

This project, presented at the Venice Biennale in 2000, was a proposal for a new type of architecture that suggested a building form with a hybrid virtual/physical presence. Oosterhuis suggests that a flexible skin with embedded LED elements and digital sensors would create a new type of space that would change the way we relate to architecture. It would enable us to move away from considering it to be a place, towards thinking of it as a medium where space is no longer fixed in either location or dimension.

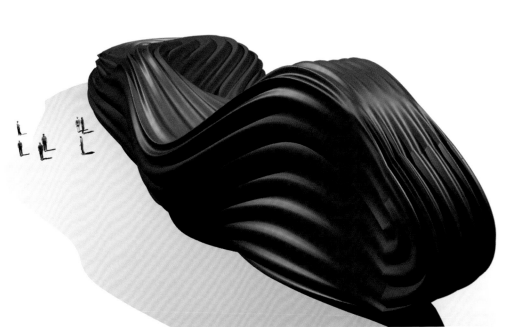

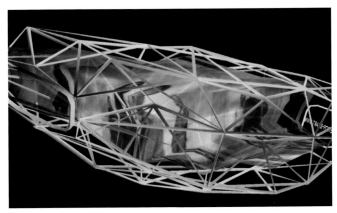

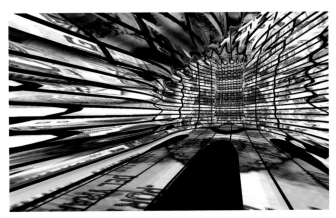

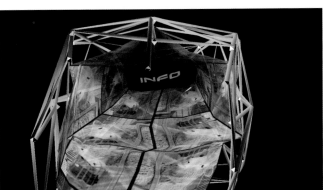

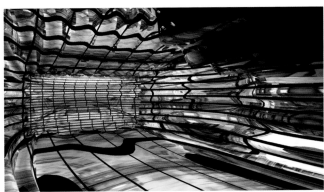

Adaptive Façade, the Netherlands,
2003: Kas Oosterhuis.

is because when physical movement decreases in ratio to
the amount of change that occurs, less energy is required to
implement that change and consequently efficiency increases.

Mechanical systems for automatic physical change are
relatively well understood in that they require motors, hinges
and actuating mechanisms, such as gears, pulleys, hydraulics or
pneumatics. Moving parts require careful construction to high
tolerances and well-programmed regular maintenance. Though
these factors do not inhibit the possibilities for interactive
design, they are counter to the idea of automatic systems,
which should ideally be self-monitoring and self-maintaining.
Nevertheless, development in this area continues to take place.

The south façade of Jean Nouvel's Arab World Institute
(1989) in Paris, France is designed in reference to the traditional
sunscreens of Arabic architecture, but with a contemporary
technological reinterpretation. The 60 metre (197 foot) high
building is a cultural and commercial showcase for the Arab
world built on a prominent site on the banks of the River
Seine. Its façade utilizes a system of mechanical shutters
that operate like the lens of a camera, opening and closing
to filter light and heat in direct response to the sun's power.

A more recent project with the same purpose, but a
completely different mechanism, has reduced the number of
moving parts considerably. The German company Festo KG,
which created the Airquarium and Airtecture (see page 202),

Adaptive Façade, the Netherlands, 2003: Kas Oosterhuis.

has developed the Fluidic Muscle – a silicon-coated, polyamide rubber tube with steel valves at each end. This device is an actuator without moving parts that causes linear movement as it expands and contracts using compressed air. Architect and designer Kas Oosterhuis has developed a concept that utilizes this device to create the Adaptive Façade (2003). This is a design for a sunshade that is more economic in material and maintenance costs, but also more interactive and dynamic in operation. Oosterhuis suggests the Fluidic Muscles can be used in conjunction with an inflatable cushion-shading device, fitted to the external skin of the building. Each muscle can be operated independently, allowing different internal spaces to experience different environments. This also dramatically affects the character of the façade, which may change from moment to moment as the sun passes across it or as people alter their requirements for the shading device.

Assembled, non-moving systems that operate either through direct control or automatically can take a number of forms. The guiding principle, however, is that once assembled and placed in position they create change without the need for physical movement of building parts. Again, in order for the architecture to be interactive, a sensing of the environment or the user's needs should bring about the changes rather than a predetermined pattern created by

Tower of Winds, Yokohama, Japan,
1986: Toyo Ito.

Tower of Winds, Yokohama, Japan,
1986: Toyo Ito.

Daycaster, Exeter, UK, 2004:
Sutherland Hussey Architects.

Interact

the architect or some other third party. It is in this area of design where applications are quickly moving from the exploratory to regular implementation.

In 1986, the Japanese architect Toyo Ito created a small project in Yokohama, Japan that exemplified the potential impact of buildings where the identity could be shifted and morphed using simple interactive visual technology. The Tower of Winds is a housing for a water tower and a ventilation shaft at the entrance to a railway station at a busy interchange where cars, buses and taxis circulate. The tower is clad in a perforated metal skin containing 1,300 lamps, which as darkness falls respond to the changing direction and strength of the wind to provide a mysterious and fascinating light show in a busy and confusing location. Artificial lights that interact with the weather have also been used by Sutherland Hussey Architects to create the Daycaster (2004), a gateway sculpture to the city of Exeter where the UK Meteorological Office had recently relocated. The structure is a 40 metre (131 foot) long metal wing shape that reflects the lights that are angled up from magenta, green and blue LEDs set into the ground below it. Weather information is sorted at the nearby office and transmitted wirelessly to the sculpture's computer, which transforms the data into a coloured pattern for each of its 24 sections (these each represent one hour of the previous day's weather).

A lighting project that responds to individuals rather than environments has been created for Jean Nouvel's 2003 Hotel Puerta America in Madrid, Spain. The walls in the hotel's eighth-floor lobby use sensors that 'see' the colours of passers-by and reflect them, chameleon-like, on their surface. Movement is also captured in this experience: someone running through the lobby will register a brief streak, while a person who stands still registers as a much stronger colour image.

Though we are accustomed to experiencing buildings in a visual way they can also interact with us in other ways, through other senses or communication devices that we carry with us. For example, people who use hearing aids are able to pick up information in many buildings through hearing loops. Dutch architect Lars Spuybroek is principal of NOX, a Rotterdam-based practice specializing in exploratory design that examines the relationship between media, computing and architecture. The practice has realized a number of projects that break down the boundaries of conventional built form, examining the potential for more fluid states of inhabitation. In 1997, they created a water pavilion for the Dutch Ministry of Transport and Waterworks at the Delta Expo on the island of Neeltje Jans in Zeeland, the Netherlands. The H2O eXPO building is a physical embodiment of 'liquid' architecture where wall, floor and ceiling surfaces fuse into a complete territory without

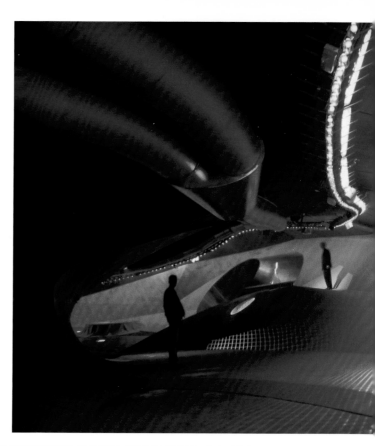

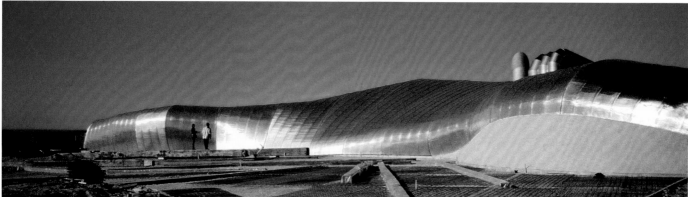

H2O eXPO, the Netherlands,
1997: NOX.

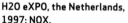

Son-O-House, the Netherlands,
2004: NOX.

Pika Pika Façade, Tokyo, Japan,
1999: Klein Dytham architecture.

boundaries. This is a place that compels individuals to react to it, in a sense 'falling' through the deformed space. The Son-O-House (2004), a permanent art installation in Son en Breugel, the Netherlands, also compels people to react to it. The swirling, twisting structure uses sensors to identify the movement of visitors and to generate corresponding sound patterns. As a visitor approaches, the ambient sound changes in reaction to their presence and, although the noise has been programmed by artist Edwin van der Heide, each visitor's experience is uniquely their own as they can influence the form it takes.

Klein Dytham architecture are a Tokyo-based practice whose work ranges far outside the normal confines of building design. They have created furniture, products, interiors and, most intriguingly, hoardings for building sites that seek to engage public involvement in the process going on behind them. In 1999 they created the Pika Pika (which means shiny in Japanese) Pretzel hoarding for developer VELOQX on the first phase of a large building site in Tokyo. Printed across the large screen was the single Japanese word *sumimasen* – sorry. In the second phase the hoarding underwent a metamorphosis as a large, perforated, translucent, metallic extension that could be illuminated from within at night was inflated above the solid wall. Pika Pika generated a large amount of publicity for the developer and consequently, in 2000, the practice was commissioned to design another hoarding, this time for Virgin Atlantic.

For this new project, the iFly Virgin Wonderwall in Tokyo, Japan, they wanted to incorporate a truly interactive device so they created the idea of installing a 20 metre (66 foot) long LED ticker-tape sign that asked a different general knowledge question each hour of the day. Passers-by could text the Virgin website with their answer and every hour all the correct entries went into a prize draw – the successful winner was notified by text. This was the first time that mobile phone technology had been used in such an interactive, location-specific manner. Since then this sort of interactivity has become far more common and will certainly become more sophisticated in the future. Chips that can access Global Positioning Satellite technology are entering mass-production, bringing their unit cost down significantly. This has enabled mobile phones to become far more location sensitive and opened up the capacity for triggering intelligent information and control systems automatically.

In 1999–2000 engineer and designer Werner Sobek built a case-study house for his family that explores the limits of contemporary building technology. The R128 House is a cubic, steel and glass volume that sits on a hillside on the edge of the vale of Stuttgart in Germany and projects into space above the city. The structure has a modular, bolt-together,

R129 House, Germany, 2001–4: Werner Sobek.

iFly Virgin Wonderwall, Tokyo, Japan, 2000: Klein Dytham architecture.

R128 House, Stuttgart, Germany, 1999–2000: Werner Sobek.

steel frame designed to be completely recyclable, with
continuous suspended glass walls on all sides of the building.
All components can be disassembled for reuse, either in the
same configuration or in a completely new building design.
The house is open plan with no partition walls and with all the
cabling and pipe work either exposed or concealed behind
easily removable, laminated metal covers, so that necessary
changes can be made with the minimum of effort – even the
bath is on wheels. The house was designed to be energy self-
sufficient and is triple-glazed using a commercial system
never before applied in housing. A heat pump system, working
in coordination with a 12,000 litre (25,360 pint) water
reservoir, balances seasonal temperature changes via
ceiling-mounted panels. On the roof there are 48 solar power
modules totalling a 6.72 kilowatt generating capacity – any
excess power is fed back into the national grid. Much of the
equipment in the house is entirely controlled via sensors and
a computer system that can be monitored through the
Internet. There are no locks or switches: the front door
operates via a voice recognition system; ambient lighting,
heating and windows are all controlled by a touch screen, but
operate automatically; and systems such as task lighting and
water taps operate by infrared sensors. The R128 House is
a forward-looking experiment with an uncompromising
architectural character that celebrates the aesthetics of

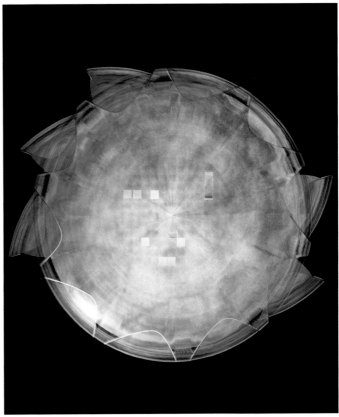

Tolvanen Cybertecture House

Denmark, 2002–4: James Law Cybertecture

Law was invited by IBM Europe and the Tolvanen Corporation to design a house that would break away from stereotypical forms of living and instead would morph in response to physical and technological needs. The project suggests a dynamic space that incorporates 'trolley' rooms that can be repositioned depending on the instructions that are given to a cyber character (a virtual butler) via a voice recognition system. The premise is that the physical space of a house could be as interactive as a personal computer interface.

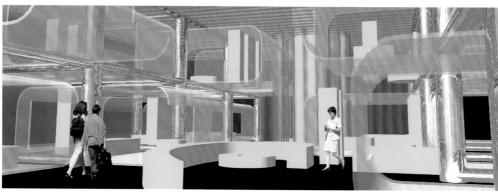

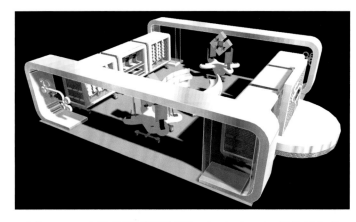

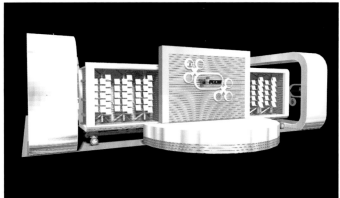

overt technology as well as its functional opportunities. The transparent, minimal, stripped-down imagery might not suit everyone, but in this case it is all the more powerful for conveying its conceptual underpinning.

Sobek has designed a follow-up prototypical project, the R129 House, that pursues his ideas about minimal use of materials, complete recyclability and self-sufficiency in energy supply. This concept achieves interactivity by utilizing new materials that are essentially solid-state but still change in response to instructions or situations. The R129 House has a plastic skin that is bonded with an electrochromatic foil, which is controlled electronically to change light transmittance when needed for privacy or shading, and solar cells, which, although they reduce light transmission by just 20 per cent, supply a large part of the building's energy demand.

Can the introduction of such sophisticated sensor and control mechanisms lead to a new way of designing architecture? James Law is a Hong Kong-based designer who styles his practice as a 'cybertecture' consultancy, designing environments that have a symbiotic balance between architectural space and technology, in particular computing. He has designed a number of innovative environments that utilize responsive technology. The Pacific Century Cyberworks (PCCW) Travelling Retail Shop (2002–4) is a mobile facility designed for Hong Kong's largest telecommunications and

Pacific Century Cyberworks Connect Multimedia and Kiosk Shops, Hong Kong, 2002–4: James Law Cybertecture.

IT company. It utilizes the mobile product display trolleys that are already used in the company's existing shops and in other public places, such as shopping malls. Each trolley has an RF-id (radio frequency identity) tag, so it can be tracked by location, together with a microprocessor that logs each of the products on sale, including its price. Together with portable counters, showcases and portals to mark the shop entrance, the entire facility fits into a standard truck and is capable of being set up in under two hours.

Law's most revolutionary project, however, is the Artificial Intelligence Media Laboratory, commissioned by the Hong Kong Government. The project is a flexible built environment the shape, configuration and character of which can be changed depending on the needs of the user. Beginning in 2001, Law's practice designed a new kind of software-based artificial intelligence called SIGNAL for the project, which communicates with people via voice recognition, human presence detectors and a controller interface. Subsequently, the concept developed into full-size interactive mock-ups of a real environment in which the computer controls mechanical servos to move walls and a hydraulic floor table as well as audio-visual systems. It also controls the environment and animatronics devices.

Materials innovation is also creating dramatic possibilities for interactive building design. LiTraCon, for

Hong Kong Government RTHK Artificial Intelligence Media Laboratory, Hong Kong, 2001: James Law Cybertecture.

Croatian Pavilion, Expo 2005

Aichi, Japan, 2005: Marko Dabrović

The Croatian Pavilion introduces the distinctive identity of this recently re-emerged country to pavilion visitors by giving them a unique experience. It is intended to challenge and engage their senses with unique audio-visual and physical transformation sensations. The environment explores the theme of transition from an underwater environment to the surface of the water. Visitors cross a threshold into a darkened space where their movements appear to generate underwater ripples. The impression of being in an underwater world is heightened by a visual and audio landscape created by five IR (infrared) illuminators, three cameras and four projectors. When visitors are gathered at the end of the floor a large platform lifts them above the 'surface' of the water into a bright sunny day with Mediterranean winds and flying kites. The light then dims before the entire set becomes a screen for a film about Croatia.

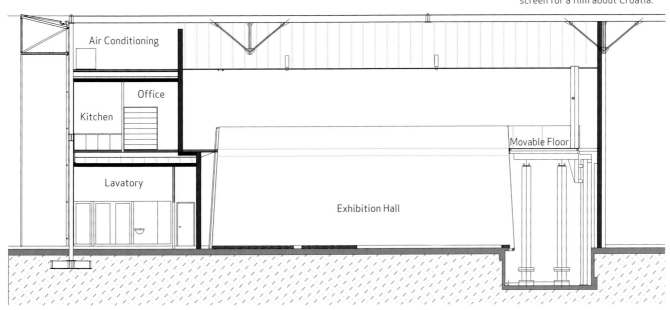

Air Conditioning

Office

Kitchen

Lavatory

Movable Floor

Exhibition Hall

Interact

example, is a transparent concrete that incorporates glass fibres 70 micrometres (0.003 of an inch) across. This enables solid walls up to 20 centimetres (7.9 inches) thick to be translucent enough for people and objects to be detected on the other side. Nanogel is another transparent material that encloses oxygen atoms in tiny spheres of bonded silicon that make up just 5 per cent of the total mass. It is extremely insulative and also hydrophobic, making it an incredibly useful material to reduce thermal transmission in façade systems where transparency and high performance is required. Macro Fibre Composite is another example of material innovation. It is a very thin (180 micrometre) piezoceramic plate that, when connected to an electric current, expands without cracking. It is used as a remote sensor, for example to warn of stress in critical building or bridge structures, because when a force is applied to the plate it will also generate a small electric charge.

Perhaps the most flexible innovation is SmartWrap, a 1 millimetre (0.04 of an inch) thick, composite building skin material that can be customized project by project to replace conventional built-up construction and also perform in a wide range of additional interactive ways. Created by Philadelphia-based architects Kieran Timberlake Associates, in association with science company DuPont, SmartWrap is based on a polyester film substrate that provides protection from external weather conditions and also forms a base onto

SmartWrap Building, New York, USA, 2003: Kieran Timberlake Associates.

which a range of other characteristics can be applied, including climate control, power supply, lighting and information display.

Climate control is implemented by Phase Change Materials (PCMs) which are microcapsules embedded into a polyester resin and then extruded into a film. PCMs work on the principle that when a substance reaches a certain temperature it changes phase (between solid, liquid or gas), which exchanges heat. A change from liquid to solid results in a release of heat, and a change from solid to liquid results in absorption of heat. PCMs are used to absorb climatic heat when the temperature is high and release it when the temperature drops. Lighting and information display is implemented by organic, light-emitting diode display (OLED). OLEDs are based on organic molecules that emit light when an electric current is applied and are either made in polymer form or small molecules that can be deposited directly onto the polymer substrate. OLEDs have lower energy use and better resolution, and are thinner and flexible in comparison to current flat-screen displays. Power supply is provided using innovative organic photo-voltaics that convert light (photons) into a steady stream of electricity (electrons), then transfer them to a coating of Buckminsterfullerene (C60) in order to sustain the OLED system. These layers are then transferred to the SmartWrap substrate using

a continuous roll-printing system called 'Deposition
Printing' that is similar to inkjet printing. Different layers
of SmartWrap can also be laminated together in a rapid
automated system for factory production.

Although all the technology that is used in SmartWrap
is proven, its transition into full manufacturing capability is
still underway. A prototype building was built for the Cooper
Hewitt Museum in New York in 2003, however, as an exemplar
of the potential of the material. It also incorporated an
exhibition showing the principles behind its design and
manufacture. The SmartWrap created for the pavilion had
an effective thermal R-value of 1.5, which is comparable to
a conventional concrete block and brick cavity wall with a
5 centimetre (2 inch) airspace and 5 centimetre (2 inch)
expanded polystyrene insulation, though with just one-
hundredth of its weight.

Interactive architecture is still an emerging area of
design. Inspiration for its development, however, is coming
from technology transfer applications where products are
already being used successfully in other industries – for
example, Macro Fibre Composites are used by Volkswagen
to reduce drumming noise caused by vibration in the roofs of
their cars by stiffening the material in response to movement.
With developments in product design, interactive architecture
is improving the range, control and responsiveness of building

functions – for example, the use of WAP-enabled mobile phones to control remote devices via the Internet. However, it is also generating its own areas of innovation such as SmartWrap, driven through industry-based research primarily by manufacturers such as DuPont or interested designers like Werner Sobek and Kieran Timberlake.

Interactive design is essentially a result of developing technologies that are making possible new and better constructional and operational strategies. The aim of these improvements is to make architecture more efficient and sustainable, and also to make the user's relationship with their built environment more comfortable and responsive. Human engagement with the built environment relates closely to issues of understanding and control. There is no doubt that interactivity at least gives the impression of greater control because the building's systems are designed to be responsive to the user's needs. However, it remains to be seen what impact it has on our understanding of architecture because automatic, sensor-controlled systems are not suited to everyone. Their mysterious quality, the presence of an unseen hand controlling our environment, can be perceived as undermining direct human decision-making. Undoubtedly there is a balance to be struck here, but until the full possibilities of interactive architecture are clear we may not be able to decide where that balance lies.

SmartWrap Building, New York, USA, 2003: Kieran Timberlake Associates.

Selected Bibliography

Adaptable Architecture, K. Kramer Publishers, 1985

Alexander, Tzonis, *Santiago Calatrava – The Complete Works*, Rizzoli, New York, 2004

Ashby, Michael and Johnson, Kara, *Materials and Design: The Art and Science of Material Selection in Product Design*, Butterworth-Heinemann, Oxford, 2000

Bell, Jonathan (ed.), 'The Transformable House', *Architectural Design*, profile no.146, vol.70, no.4, Wiley-Academy, London, 2000

Brayer, Marie-Ange and Migayrou, Frederic (eds.), *Archilab: Radical Experiments in Global Architecture*, Thames and Hudson, London, 2001

Brayer, Marie-Ange and Simonot, Beatrice (eds.), *Archilab's Earth Buildings: Radical Experiments in Land Architecture*, Thames and Hudson, London, 2003

Brookes, Alan J. and Poole, Dominique (eds.), *Innovation in Architecture*, Spon Press, London and New York, 2004

Burkhart, Bryan and Hunt, David, *Airstream: The History of the Land Yacht*, Chronicle Books, San Francisco, 2000

Cole, Barbara and Rogers, Ruth (eds.), *Richard Rogers Architects, Architectural Monographs*, Academy Editions, London, 1985

Constant, Caroline and Wang, Wilfred (eds.), *Eileen Gray: An Architecture for All Senses*, Deutsches Architektur-Museum, Frankfurt-am-Main, Harvard Graduate School of Design, Cambridge, Mass., Wasmuth, Berlin, 1996

Cook, Peter (ed.), *Archigram*, Studio Vista, London, 1972

Crosbie, Nick, *I'll Keep Thinking*, Black Dog Publishing, London and New York, 2003

Davies, Colin, *The Prefabricated Home*, Reaktion Books, Trowbridge, 2005

Eaton, Ruth, *Ideal Cities: Utopianism and the (Un)Built Environment*, Thames and Hudson, London, 2001

Flexible Spaces (Architecture Showcase), Links International, 2004

Frampton, Kenneth, *Steven Holl: Architect*, Phaidon, London, 2003

Friedman, Avi and Grillo, Scott (eds.), *The Adaptable House: Designing Homes for Change*, McGraw-Hill Education, 2002

Galfetti, Gustau Gili, *Model Apartments: Experimental Domestic Cells*, Editorial Gustavo Gili, Barcelona, 1997

Garofalo, Francesco, *Steven Holl*, Thames and Hudson, London, 2003

Gassmann, O. and Meixner, H. (eds.), *Sensors in Intelligent Buildings*, Wiley-VCH, Weinheim, 2001

Habraken, John, *The Structure of the Ordinary: Form and Control in the Built Environment*, ed. Jonathan Teicher, MIT Press, Cambridge, Mass., and London, 1998

Habraken, John, *Supports: An Alternative to Mass Housing* (1961), Urban Press, Seattle, 1999

Hartoonian, Gevark, *Ontology of Construction: On Nihilism of Technology in Themes of Modern Architecture*, Harvard University Press, Cambridge, Mass., 1994

Herwig, Oliver, *Featherweights: Light, Mobile and Floating Architecture*, Prestel, Munich, 2003

Hoete, Anthony (ed.), *Roam: Reader on the Aesthetics of Mobility*, Black Dog Publishing, London and New York, 2004

Jackson, Neil, *The Modern Steel House*, E&FN Spon, London, 1996

Jandl, H. Ward, *Yesterday's Houses of Tomorrow: Innovative American Homes 1850–1950*, Preservation Press, Washington, DC, 1991

Jencks, Charles and Baird, George (eds.), *Meaning in Architecture*, George Braziller, New York, 1969

Kendall, Stephen and Teicher, Jonathan, *Residential Open Building*, E&FN Spon, London and New York, 2000

Kieran, Stephen and Timberlake, James, *Refabricating Architecture: How Manufacturing Methodologies are Poised to Transform Building Construction*, McGraw-Hill (Higher Education), New York, 2004

Krausse, Joachim and Lichtenstein, Claud, *Your Private Sky: R. Buckminster Fuller, Art of Design Science/Your Private Sky: Discourse*, Lars Müller Publishers, Baden, 1999

David Krell (ed.), *Martin Heidegger, Basic Writings*, Routledge, London, 1993

Kronenburg, Robert, *Houses in Motion: The History, Development and Potential of the Portable Building*, second edition, Wiley-Academy, Chichester, 2002

Kronenburg, Robert, *Portable Architecture*, third edition, Architectural Press, Oxford, 2003

Kronenburg, Robert, *Spirit of the Machine: Technology as an Influence on Architectural Form*, Wiley-Academy, Chichester, 2001

Kronenburg, Robert and Klassen, Filiz (eds.), *Transportable Environments III*, E&FN Spon, London and New York, 2005

Lang, Peter and Menking, William, *Superstudio: Life without Objects*, Skira Editore SpA., Milan, 2003

Leach, Neal, Turnbull, David and Williams, Chris (eds.), *Digital Techtonics*, Wiley-Academy, London. 2004

Lefebvre, Henri, *Everyday Life in the Modern World*, Transaction, New Brunswick, 1999

Lüchinger, Arnulf (ed.), *Herman Hertzberger: Buildings and Projects*, Arch-Edition, The Hague, 1987

Lupton, Ellen, *Skin: Surface, Substance and Design*, Laurence King, London, 2002

Maffei, Andrea, *Toyo Ito: Works Projects Writings*, Electa Architecture, Milan, 2002

Melis, Liesbeth, *Parasite Paradise: A Manifesto For Temporary Architecture and Flexible Urbanism*, NAi Publishers, Rotterdam, 2003

Mollerup, Per, *Collapsibles: A Design Album of Space-saving Objects*, Thames and Hudson, London, 2001

Mori, Toshiko (ed.), *Immaterial/Ultramaterial: Architecture, Design and Materials*, Harvard Design School in association with George Braziller, New York, 2002

Motro, René, *Tensegrity: Structural Systems for the Future*, Butterworth-Heinemann, Oxford, 2003

Nitschke, Günter, *From Shinto to Ando: Studies in Architectural Anthropology in Japan*, Academy, London, 1993

Oliver, Paul, *Shelter and Society*, Barrie and Rockliff, London, 1969

Pope, Nicolas, *Experimental Houses*, Laurence King, London, 2000

Rapoport, Amos, *House Form and Culture*, Prentice Hall, Englewood Cliffs, New Jersey, 1969

Reeser, Amanda and Schafer, Ashley, 'New Technologies://New Architectures', *Praxis*, issue 6, Cambridge, Mass., 2004

Riley, Terence, *Light Construction*, Museum of Modern Art, New York, 1995

Riley, Terence, *The Un-private House*, Museum of Modern Art, New York, 1999

Ronconi, Luca (ed.), 'Temporary', *Lotus International*, no.122, Milan, November 2004

Rudofsky, Bernard, *Architecture Without Architects*, Museum of Modern Art, New York, 1964

Rybczynski, Witold, *Home: A Short History of an Idea*, Penguin, New York, 1987

St John Wilson, Colin, *The Other Tradition of Modern Architecture: The Uncompleted Project*, Academy Editions, London, 1995

Schwartz-Clauss, Mathias (ed.), *Living in Motion: Design and Architecture for Flexible Dwelling*, Vitra Design Museum, Weil-am-Rhein, 2002

Siegal, Jennifer (ed.), *Mobile: The Art of Portable Architecture*, Princeton Architectural Press, New York, 2002

Stuhlmacher, Mechtild and Korteknie, Rien (eds.), *The City of Small Things*, Stichting Parasite Foundation, Rotterdam, 2001

Topham, Sean, *Move House*, Prestel, London, 2004

Zellner, Peter, *Hybrid Space: New Forms in Digital Architecture*, Thames and Hudson, London, 1999

Index